· Close But No Cigar ·

· Close But No Cigar ·

30 wonderful years with
GEORGE BURNS

BY MELISSA MILLER

NewStar
press

ISBN 0-7871-1291-7

Printed in the United States of America

NewStar Press
8955 Beverly Boulevard
Los Angeles, CA 90048
(310) 786-1600

Text design by Carolyn Wendt
Cover design by Rick Penn-Kraus

First Printing: May 1998

10 9 8 7 6 5 4 3 2 1

*This book is, of course, dedicated to George Burns.
But without the multifaceted love of my husband, Paul,
and our sons, "The Fabulous Berry Bros."—Nathaniel and Benjamin—
and the enduring friendships of Jo-Ann, Mollie, Tonda, Stephen,
Max, and Jay, I never would have had the ability to
follow through on this project.*

—**M.M.**

· PROLOGUE ·

What do an eighteen-year-old girl and a seventy-one-year-old man have in common? Everything. At least that was the case with George Burns and me when we met in 1967.

Ever since then, at one time or another, he and I lived together, worked together, traveled together, argued together, and occasionally separated, only to come back together—and always with a great love. He was my "best fella," best friend, mentor, and role model for "unconditional love," which was a foreign concept to me until I met him.

As I was growing up, my mother convinced me that mediocrity was the best I could hope to achieve in anything. And I believed it until I was eighteen, at which point I met my own personal guardian angel—George Burns. He told me I was the best and the brightest. Throughout the years, he told me hundreds of things about me and about the world that gave me courage and fortitude to believe in myself and the choices I've made. He told me to find what it was I loved the most and do it. No matter what, he'd say, "Stick with it, Kid, even if it's making ladies' felt hats."

GB also convinced me that I had something my mother didn't recognize. I had gotten some recessive gene from our family woodpile—"something" that he had assured me over the decades was more subtle and enduring than early physical beauty, academic success, or prodigious talent, which everyone in my family seemed to have but me. I had spunk, resiliency, curiosity, a slightly "off-center" sense of humor (his words), and the ability to land on my feet (size 10 and the butt of numerous family jokes). He taught me that with these qualities it was possible to become pretty, talented, desirable, educated beyond one's intelligence, musically gifted, domesticated (tamed), *ad infinitum.* And he was right. But he also tempered his love and support for me by occasionally reminding me, "Kid, you're not easy."

GB was right about that. And he was also right when he repeatedly told me, "Kid, I'm the nicest man you'll ever meet."

That's why you, the reader, might consider *Close But No Cigar* the world's longest love letter to the world's nicest man.

I began to assemble this album of personal photographs, letters, and stories of our thirty-year friendship several years ago as a gift for GB in anticipation of his 100th birthday. However, shortly after his ninety-eighth birthday, his health started to fail, and I began seriously sorting through, assembling, and making personal notes on all the material.

Every week when I went to spend time with him, as I had in so many ways for so many years, I started bringing him different bits of memorabilia of our life together to reminisce over. It wasn't always easy during this period. Thirty years is a long time and to know we didn't have another thirty years was overwhelmingly sad for me. But reliving our adventures together always seemed to rekindle the spark in his eyes that toward the end seemed so dim. And on these occasions, when GB pored over the souvenirs of our life together with such delight, the impending sense of loss I'd someday share with the world was lessened.

· O N E ·

*"Kid, you don't have to be so
strong when you say no. . . . It just
makes it that much harder if you
ever want to change it to a yes."*

June 1994, Beverly Hills

As I slowly climb the circular stairs at 720 North Maple for the umpteenth time in nearly thirty years, I dread what I have imagined will be a devastating scene in the master bedroom.

Hospital bed, IVs dripping, bedpans, medications lined up on trays, plastic pitchers of warm water, flex-straws, catheters, oxygen tanks.

By the time all this runs through my head I've arrived at *his* bedroom door, which

I've found ajar. What will I say? Can I keep from crying? Will he have trouble recognizing me?

I timidly push the half-opened door.

Oh my God! There's no one there and the bed is made up militarily "crisp." The room starts to spin in front of my eyes, until I hear, "Hey, Kid. Over here."

He's sitting at his desk! The windows behind him allow the morning sun to create the aura of a halo around his frail body and his sweetly bald head, and he glows. Gee, maybe his series of *Oh, God!* movies weren't so far-fetched after all. How else could he be sitting there at this point in time still wearing that trademark smile, those round glasses, and, of course, that ever-present cigar with that ringed pinky finger delicately held aloft?

"GB! You look great! In fact, you look terrific!"

"Yeah, really?"

"Yeah, really!"

I move toward him for our usual smooch, but he tilts his face up to me for a kiss on the lips rather than the standard one on the top of his head that has come to be our greeting over the last couple of years. He *is* feeling better. And kissing him on the lips so soundly reassures me that the dream isn't over yet. He's still here. And he's still the best.

I pull away so we're just eye to eye and nose to nose, and grin at him because I'll always be the smitten eighteen-year-old he met all those years ago. As usual, he grins back.

"It's good to see you, Kid."

"Yeah, it's good to see you, too."

As I sit down across from him, I casually ask, "So GB, what's new?" He gets that familiar glint in his eyes that he saves for me and responds, "Take a look at me, Kid. Does anything look new?" Once again, he's right!

Luckily, the cookies and tea are served right then and we can temporarily change our focus. The tea is boiling hot (the same way he likes his soup) and the cookies are neatly laid out on a silver tray. Now, GB has never been a big "knife-and-fork man," as he says—in other words, he's not much interested in food. I look at all these cookies and hit him with a line out of an old Burns and Allen routine from the '30s called "Lamb Chops." Food jokes were a big item during the Depression. The routine is what's known as a "man and woman" act, which is how Burns and Allen started. The part of the routine I always remember goes like this:

GEORGE
Let me ask you something. Do you like to take walks?

GRACIE
No.

GEORGE
Well, gee. Do you like to dance?

GRACIE
No.

GEORGE
Well, what do you like?

GRACIE

Lamb chops.

GEORGE

Lamb chops! Well, let me ask you something else. Can a little girl like you eat two big lamb chops all alone?

GRACIE

No, but with potatoes I could.

GEORGE

One more thing. Would you like to kiss?

GRACIE

No. But I'd like it if you'd walk me home.

GEORGE

Is your mother home?

GRACIE

Of course, but my father won't let you kiss my mother.

So I ask, "GB, can you eat that whole big plate of cookies all alone?"

The glint reappears in his eyes, there is a slow take, and he responds, "No, but with hot tea I could."

Yeah, he's going to be okay.

As he eats his cookies, we start to talk about the move I made the previous week. I've separated from my second husband after sixteen years and am now living by myself because our two young sons live with their father. Of course, GB prefaces his next question with a droll, "Y'know, Kid, you're not easy." Then, with no segue, he asks me, "So, how *are* Paul and the boys doing?"

Uh-oh, here we go. He's going to tell me yet another time what a wonderful father, husband, and provider Paul is and that he hopes I haven't made another one of my "putzy" mistakes by separating from a second perfectly good husband.

So before this conversation can continue, I bring up the topic that I know will always distract him: show business.

"Y'know GB, I bet you'll play Vegas for your ninety-ninth birthday after all."

"I don't know, Kid. I can't see myself making an entrance. The walk on stage could finish me off."

"But GB, what if they opened the curtains to reveal you sitting in a swell, overstuffed chair with your cigar? You change the opening joke: 'I used to be able to do everything standing up—now I do everything sitting down . . . even some things I never could do standing up.'"

"That's not a good finish to that joke."

"Poppa (as my two young sons call him)! It was just off the top of my head."

"Well, then you'd better have your head looked at!"

"Whatever."

"No, not *whatever*."

Wait a minute. We're right back at each other, just like old times. This is the person

I've loved in every possible way the most consistently for two-thirds of my life. This is the person who gently and generously prodded me into adulthood and independence at the expense of possibly losing me; listened to me whine and kvetch my way through two marriages that in reality had very little wrong with them except that I was a participant; watched me "shoot myself in the foot" repeatedly in various professional situations because of my own stubbornness; and yet always, always let me throw my arms around his neck and sob piteously when life and its realities were just more than I could bear, always ending my tears with, "Come on, Kid, dinner's here and the soup's gonna get cold."

This is the person who had been playing bridge with the Grim Reaper for the last two weeks after the doctors drilled two holes in his skull to relieve fluid buildup. And now he wants to change the punch lines for his January '95 birthday party at Caesar's Palace and tell me about my bad jokes!

Five more minutes pass as we enthusiastically discuss his act, and suddenly he's ready for a nap. I leave feeling a million times better than when I arrived. He's going to be okay. He really *is* going to be okay. I'm not going to lose him after all. At least not while he's still booked in show business.

I get in my car and start home with only thoughts of him on my mind.

Two Weeks Later

GB's children have been visiting and making decisions about what the "proper health care" will be. Irving, his longtime manager, still hasn't canceled any of GB's bookings so I imagine the "proper health care" will be what GB has always advised: "The first thing ya gotta do, Kid, is get out of bed in the morning." I know that as long as he's booked he'll always get out of bed.

He *is* looking better and better. It's like old times . . . almost. He's back going to the office, going to Hillcrest for lunch and playing cards for a bit afterward, and I'm back fixing him martinis whenever I come to visit. I think about how amazing he is but realize that I would never expect anything less of him because he's never expected anything less of himself.

My sons, Nathaniel (Nathan Birnbaum's namesake) and Ben, have come with me for the first time since their "Poppa" got sick. I am not quite sure what it will be like for them because they are only six and ten and have never really seen anyone who's been seriously ill.

The boys cautiously approach him instead of making their usual mad dash for a kiss, a hug, and a slurp of his martini. I realize that he really doesn't look much different. He sits there with his cigar, martini, pajamas, robe, slippers, and no hair—everything just like it always is when we come for dinner every week.

They turn and look at me as if I'd told them an enormous lie! One of them says to me, "He still looks just like Poppa!"

GB looks at me and asks, "What'd he say?"

I smile, knowing what his take will be. "He says you look just the same."

"Of course I look the same. I'm too old to look any different!"

With this the boys rush over. GB reaches out and puts an arm around each one and gives them each their usual kiss and squeeze. They both eyeball his martini.

GB looks up at me and commands, "Kid, get them some olives and onions from the bar." I return with a small napkin loaded with cocktail onions and pimiento-stuffed olives and set it all in front of him. GB enthusiastically dunks a cocktail onion into his gin and pops it into Nathaniel's mouth as my son stands there expectantly with his mouth open like a baby bird. Ben is next and chooses an olive. Another dunk, and GB's fingers pop it into Ben's mouth. With this done, he tells them to get themselves some nuts from the nut dish and help themselves to a chocolate from the candy dish. It is the chocolates that always give me pause. The candy dish is an irreplaceable piece of Steuben crystal from the '30s which they haven't yet broken (and they never did!). With the opening ritual of our dinner complete, there is only one thing left: The boys should go to the pool and take a swim and leave us alone!

"You've got two beautiful boys there, Kid."

"Thanks, GB."

"It looks like Paul is doing a good job with them."

I tell him, yet again, that I think Paul is a terrific father, very talented, and a nice man—but not a great husband. End of discussion, I hope. And then, without missing a beat he reminds me, "Y'know kid, I could have been your first husband. Aren't you glad you didn't marry me?"

I used to think that I was, but now I'm not sure. We almost got married on several occasions, the first being only months after GB and I first met. I was eighteen.

■ ■ ■ ■ ■ ■ ■ ■ ■ ■ ■ ■ ■ ■ ■

Eighteen. At eighteen, I'd never been out of the state of California. I'd never really even been away from home. I'd been brought up by my mother from the time I was five with the help of my mother's parents "Nana" and "Gumpy," and her sister, my wonderful Aunt Noël. During this whole time of growing up there were several constants in my life that would eventually have a great deal to do with meeting GB and our ensuing friendship.

My family always stressed the importance of getting a good education, which definitely included having an appreciation of music. At an early age I started piano lessons. During the summers I lived with my grandparents. Nana taught me everything she ever knew about light opera and ragtime tunes. Her knowledge was considerable, since she'd spent her early years as a "song plugger" in downtown Los Angeles. (A song plugger was a piano player who'd play and sing the latest songs in front of the music stores to get people to buy the newest popular sheet music.)

Little did Nana realize how teaching me all this would shape my life. Because of the love of music she passed on to me, I started auditioning for local musicals. By the time I was eighteen, I'd been singing and dancing in musicals at the Civic Light Opera for several years and could play or sing most ragtime pieces from the early part of the century! But none of this dissuaded my family from insisting that getting an education was the number-one priority.

Nonetheless, I auditioned for a professional singing job at the end of my first year of college. It was for a group called the Kids Next Door, which was an offshoot of the Young Americans. I got the job!

I'd started taking college courses while I was still in high school so at the time of this audition I'd already completed one year of college and was, theoretically, a year ahead of myself in school. When I got the job to go on the road with the group, I went. The group ended its spring tour as GB's opening act in Vegas. Looking back, I guess that's when my "life" tour with GB began.

Everyone in the group was so excited that we would be at the Riviera Hotel in Las Vegas opening for George Burns. I really didn't even know who he was. I vaguely remembered that he'd had a TV show with his wife, Gracie, when I was really little. He'd spy on her from a special TV in his office and then talk directly to the audience. She was always smarter than he was—or so it seemed. The road manager told us that Gracie had passed away about three years earlier from a heart attack and warned us not to say anything about her or *The Burns and Allen Show* unless Mr. Burns mentioned it first. That didn't seem too tall an order since I hadn't planned on talking to him anyway.

For some odd reason, things have very rarely gone the way I've planned. That month in Vegas was no exception. During this engagement, GB had a "dresser" named Charlie Reid. Charlie Reid was an old vaudevillian who was out of work, so GB gave him a job taking care of his wardrobe and keeping things together. Charlie loved to chat and I liked to listen. One evening before the show, Charlie explained to me that he'd been a "hoofer," as had GB initially, and that's how they'd met. I told him how much I loved tap dancing and we started comparing time steps and different riffs.

It was during one of our tapping sessions in the hall that GB heard us and came out to see what was going on. There we were, doing "triple time steps." He came over to me and asked me if I could do a "traveling time step" and gave me a push on the arm to show me how to do it. I, in return, reached over and twisted his nose between my thumb and forefinger and suggested that he not poke me in the arm! We locked eyes. His eyes screwed up and got what would become that all-too-familiar "glint." I told him I didn't know a traveling time step. He asked me if I knew the song "Willie the Weeper." I said no again. He asked what I knew about show business and I told him I knew how to play "The Maple Leaf Rag."

"I got a piano. Why don't you come in and play it?"

I sat down at the spinet in his dressing room and proceeded to play the first thirty-two bars.

I stopped, turned around grinning, and looked at him smugly. He asked me if I wanted to go out to dinner. I said a definite no. And then he said something to me that he would end up saying to me for the next thirty years: "Kid, you don't have to be so strong when you say no because I don't think anyone's ever going to make you do anything you don't want to. Besides, it just makes it that much harder when you want to change it to a yes." What he said made a big impression on me because it was the first time someone had ever corrected me in a way that made sense and was constructive.

I didn't go back to see Charlie Reid for tapping the next night. There was something about it all that I couldn't explain, at least not at eighteen, but I somehow knew if I did go back I'd be learning a traveling time step and then some.

After a couple of nights of not tapping with Charlie, one of the guys from the group came looking for me. He told me that Mr. Burns wanted to see me. I asked him why and he looked at me as if I had two heads and just walked away. I trudged upstairs, of course assuming that I was going to get into trouble for something innocuous since I'd been getting in trouble at home for innocuous things most of my life.

GB was sitting in his dressing room with Charlie. I knocked on the open door and he gave me "the glint" and "the grin."

"What's the problem, Kid?"

"What do you mean?"

"I mean you haven't come to visit for a couple of nights. I only see you onstage."

"I don't know a traveling time step," I replied sarcastically.

"You don't know 'Willie the Weeper,' either."

Finally we just smiled at each other.

"Come on in and keep us company."

I hesitatingly went in and sat down. He asked me if Charlie could get me something to drink. It was all very different than it had been and very unsettling. Then he had his piano player come up and play "Willie the Weeper." The rest is history. Ours, anyway. I learned the traveling time step *and* "Willie the Weeper"!

(Sung to the tune of "Minnie the Moocher")

You ever hear the story about Willie the Weeper?
Willie the Weeper was a chimney sweeper.
Well, he got the dope habit
And he got it bad
Listen, and I'll tell you all the dreams he had.

Dreamed he had a barrel of diamond rings and money
Mamas by the score to love and call him honey.
Everywhere he went the people all would say:
"There's the guy who put the 'B' in old Broadway."

Went to London town, bought the Picadilly
Told the people there that it belonged to Willie
Bought the King some ginger beer that made him rave
Called him "Uncle George" and said, "You need a shave."

CHORUS:
And in the morning when the lights are low,
That's when Willie gets that happy glow
And now poor Willie, he's in a trance
Cause he's gotta have that stuff and without it he can't dance.

Some song, huh? Of course, at the time I really had no idea what it was about, but it was fun to sing it with GB and do the sand dance that he taught me. I thought we were both just having some fun between shows but he had other plans for me, which were revealed shortly after I perfected the song's harmony parts and dance steps.

My girlfriend from junior high school, Susan Somerville, and her parents were coming to Vegas to see the show. I had asked GB if he could help me make sure that they had a nice table up front for the second show because they were very special friends to me. Without another word, he did just that. That night, as we were taking our bows after the Kids Next Door finished the closing medley with him, he went back to the mike and said he had a special treat. He explained that "one of the little girls" in the group had "some very special friends" in the audience and now he was going to give them a "very special treat"—and with that he called ME! up to the microphone. He offered me his hand as I approached him.

He nodded to his pianist, who played the intro to "Willie the Weeper," and we looked at each other and started to sing! There, in front of the packed main room of the Riviera Hotel, I clung to GB's hand and we sang our entire song. It certainly didn't make me popular with the other kids in the group. They all had very serious ambitions for careers in show business and all were very talented—much more than I! I had always liked being in the chorus or having a minor part, but I never wanted to be the lead in anything. Now, here I was, getting the attention they all so desperately wanted and I really didn't deserve!

The next time I had visitors I didn't tell him, but he found out anyway.

We'd started having dinner together every night after the second show, and one night I told him that I couldn't join him. He asked me what the problem was and I told him there was no problem; it was just that my mother and brother were in town to see the show and we had made other plans. He suggested that maybe they'd like to have dinner with him after the show. I told him no.

When my family came backstage after the show, he approached them himself and invited them to dinner. Much to my surprise, they accepted! By this time I was becoming entranced with him. He was so direct, funny, charming, and persistent. It was his charm that changed my life.

During dinner, he told my mother that he wanted me to work in his act doing the Burns and Allen routine. My mom said no!—I had to come back home and finish college. So he promised I'd finish college. But it still wasn't a done deal with my family. They'd had a wonderful time and he certainly was charming, but . . . no.

When we first met.

After they left, GB and I started spending all our time together. He introduced me to the card game twenty-one.

"Kid, only play with a single deck and count the cards; always insure a twenty-one; split a pair of sixes, sevens, or eights; and only let a bet ride three times when you're winning—then put it all away and go back to your two-dollar bet and start again." He also explained some card etiquette to me. If you have an obviously losing hand and the player next to you could use a card, let it go and let them have the card because you're obviously going to lose anyway and with the card you might take they might win. He also introduced me to raw oysters (which I would eat by the dozen), steak tartare, gin martinis, and Jack Benny. It was great!

The kids in the group were very envious and I couldn't blame them. I was certainly not the best-looking girl in the group. In fact, I was pretty goofy-looking. Very, very short blond hair; big, thick, square horn-rims; and a less-than-exceptional figure. And I sang flat (as the line captain of the group kept insisting in her notes after the show). But I was having a great time.

When GB's friends or family came to see the show, I was always invited to dinner afterward, followed by a trip to a lounge show—usually Shecky Green or Don Rickles.

The manager for the group told me that if I didn't stop hanging out with George Burns and gambling and drinking, I would be let go. And at the end of the month I was. But what a month it had been! And what a life was yet to come.

■ ■ ■ ■ ■ ■ ■ ■ ■ ■ ■ ■ ■ ■ ■

I had no idea what I was going to do after Vegas. I just figured I'd go back home to my mother's in Los Angeles and return to college in the fall. I figured wrong once again.

GB and I flew home together. He asked me if I'd still have dinner with him now that we were back in town. I thought that was odd. How did the town in which we lived figure into our dinner dates? Oh, I was so naive.

I worked one last gig with the Kids Next Door in Los Angeles during Fourth of July weekend, and GB and I decided that we would get together for dinner after the show. Then we started having dinner every Thursday since that was the day when his household help was off and he was on his own. My mother always came along with us and a couple of his friends or maybe his son and daughter-in-law. In the meantime, GB had gotten me to agree to play with him on his next engagement—whatever that might be. And as long as I was just waiting for school to start, why didn't I take some acting classes? And since I loved tap dancing so much, why didn't I take some dance classes?

He had Jack Langdon, who ran his office, research acting classes and find a dance teacher. GB wrote a check for both and I started.

I thought I'd died and gone to heaven. Here I had someone completely absorbed in me and my interests, convincing me that I could do anything if I worked hard enough. There was no criticism. No nagging. No arguing. Just love, support, lots and lots of laughs, and fun and goofy jokes.

In spite of all this, I wasn't feeling well. I was nauseous, tired, weak, and unable to keep any food down no matter what fabulous restaurants we frequented. By Labor Day of that summer, I was in an emergency room in Long Beach being examined and prepared for exploratory abdominal surgery. By the end of that weekend, I was in a hospital bed in Long Beach Community Hospital with an incision from hip bone to hip bone and minus my appendix and a considerable length of intestine.

GB came to Long Beach to the hospital to visit me. They even let him smoke his cigar in my room. As usual, I was oblivious to the fact that he was a celebrity. I only knew that he was my best friend at this point and that seeing him was a wonderful tonic.

During all of this, my mother had suddenly started seeing an old family friend named Lee. When it was time for me to leave the hospital, my mother and I went up to his house on the Mendocino coast.

My time with GB had become almost nonexistent and we really didn't see much of one another for the next month. In a letter to me dated September 5, 1967, he sent me a hundred-dollar bill and the following instructions:

> "Enclosed find a little something so you, your mother,
> and your brother can have a good time in San Francisco.
> This will take you to some of the good restaurants and
> you can eat some good food, because you were telling me
> the stuff at the hospital was rotten. I don't know what
> you were complaining about. Personally I think that ham
> with raisins and pineapple on it is awful. And jello is
> another one of my weaknesses. I wouldn't use that to
> put my cigar out. Anyway, have a nice time."

He went on to tell me that he was going to be at the Plaza Hotel in New York and that I should write to him (and I did). He finished the letter by signing *my* name to it! I thought that was a hilarious touch but no one else got it or ever has when I've told them about it. Inherent goofiness.

About a month later, we finally saw one another again. Before we did, he sent me yet another letter that I thought was hysterical but again no one else got it.

22

"[Here's] a letter that I got from your brother Phil and
[sister-in-law] Andi I thought maybe you'd like to see
it. It was a nice note. Your brother says, 'the foregoing
is a lie,' so your brother is also stealing my stuff.
Between you and your brother I'll have nothing left.
What am I complaining about, at my age who's got
something left anyway?"

He chats a bit more in the letter about different friends of mine that he'd met and
ended with

". . . well, I'll probably run into you one of these days
again, and I hope you recognize me. I've got new hair.
This has got to be a short note because I just called the
club and ordered some fish. And it takes them 25
minutes to burn my fish and it takes me 20 minutes to
get from my office to the club. So. . . ."

Soon after that, my mother and I were back to having our usual Thursday night
dinner with GB. One night he started grilling my mom about Lee. She finally admitted that he had asked her to marry him but she just didn't know what she was going
to do about "the baby."

By this time, I was a pretty big baby. And since she hadn't worried so very much about me before, I didn't see why it was a problem now. GB told her that after being divorced for nearly fifteen years, she should go ahead and get married again and move to Northern California and that *he* would take care of "the baby."

Of course, that was just what my mother wanted to hear. In the first week of November, she and Lee were married at my Aunt Noël's house. GB was there, as he would eventually be at all my family's events and weddings—including my own!

I started to once again dine with GB and his friends on Thursdays—but now without my mother. Since I was still living forty minutes away in Long Beach, I would usually spend the night at GB's home in the upstairs bedroom that years before had been turned into an office. The help would set up a rollaway bed for me.

We were spending more and more time together, especially since we were busy preparing for a joint appearance on *The Dean Martin Show.* Our enjoyment of one another's company super-seded everything else—including good judgment.

GB was now taking me with him to various intimate dinner parties where, after Gracie's death, he'd been particularly welcome as the "extra man." Suddenly, he was no longer the extra man, and he was

GB with friends Janet and Fred de Cordova.

dragging along this teenager to boot. I never saw it this way at all until years later. I'd always treated everyone pretty much the same until they showed me that I shouldn't, but my well-mannered yet open and forthright behavior was too frighteningly honest for most of these situations.

There were several individuals and couples who had the grace to get to know me before they dismissed me. Edward G. Robinson and his wife, Jane; Janet and Freddy de Cordova; Eddie Buzzell; and Jack and Mary Benny—to name a few—were always warm and welcoming to me, whatever their reasons. They never let me know that everyone else thought something very odd was going on. In fact, Janet and Freddy are now the only friends left from that crowd, and they gave me the most exquisite bridal dinner for my marriage to Paul.

It was during this period of being together all the time that we first started having our run-ins about getting married.

GB, half jesting, was always asking me why he and I shouldn't just get married. Sometimes I would seriously consider it, but then always after some time had elapsed I knew in my heart it wouldn't work. But that first New Year's we were together we came perilously close. We were in Vegas with Jane and Edward G. Robinson, and Jane had, unbeknownst to me (but known to GB), brought a platinum wedding band with her from Marvin Hime Jewelers.

The night before, we had seen Frank Sinatra's show, which in itself was pretty exciting. The next morning, GB suggested that after our room-service breakfast we should try to get married. There was something about the way he put it this time that made me get out the yellow pages to look up a justice of the peace.

Luckily, room service was slower than usual and I once again had time to consider the ramifications of what we were doing.

I didn't think what we were doing was wrong. I never did. I still don't. We loved each other.

An age difference? What was that? So his hair sat on a block at night. So what? He was warm and cuddly and the most affectionate and sweet human being I'd ever known.

Most people in town hadn't been too nice about us being together. But we didn't care. My family was somewhat shocked but hadn't hesitated to invite GB to all the family functions. I didn't care. My friends had quietly resigned themselves to the relationship, knowing that I usually did what I wanted anyway. Again, I didn't care. But if we were to marry, there *would* be awful things written about GB, and I did care about that. So we didn't get married.

It probably wouldn't have made any difference to us if we'd gotten married. But I have to tell you, I've always had a special affection for room service ever since.

· T W O ·

*"There's **nothing** quite so bad **as**
something not so bad."*

—George Burns & The Scarlet Pimpernel

Aside from marriage, there was only one other thing on which we didn't see eye to
eye from the beginning. From the time we'd started working together—on that
episode of *The Dean Martin Show* in 1967—rehearsing was one of our biggest
"beefs." He always wanted to rehearse and I just didn't get it.

Rehearse. My part in "the act" consisted of being introduced as a young girl who
happened to know all the Burns and Allen routines and was invited to do Gracie's part.
Luckily, I was totally ignorant of the wrath that would be provoked by *anyone* trying
to replace Gracie. The routines, to me, made perfect sense, so what was there to
rehearse? All I had to do was memorize the lines! Perhaps that was why GB asked

me to work with him. Illogical logic. A way of life for me. Because of this, when GB and I were on stage, I was totally ingenuous. And because I always trusted him completely and he had never done anything to hurt or embarrass me, when he asked me to try this material on stage, I never thought that maybe my working with him would offend someone. Nor did I realize the gift I had been given.

So, every time he wanted to rehearse, I'd tell him that I had all the lines memorized and didn't need to rehearse, to which he'd reply, "Kid, stop acting like you're Spunky Weiss! [Spunky Weiss was in Murder Inc. and was sent to the electric chair in the '30s.] If you're so smart, then how does it go?"

I'd always wait a beat and then, with a smirk, reply, "Good."

I'd always hit him with that line because it was always the one he'd use on me when I'd ask him about a classical piece of music I was learning. I'd start practicing the piano and he'd say, "Kid, I know that piece." And I'd retort, "Then how does it go?" And he'd respond, "Good!"

This time after I gave him my usual smart-aleck answer, with his gaze never leaving mine, he said, "You start."

This is the routine I still remember us doing that first time we worked together.

GEORGE BURNS–LISA MILLER
THE DEAN MARTIN SHOW

GEORGE
The last time I played Vegas at the Riviera Hotel, there was a group on the bill called the Kids Next Door.

There was one girl in the group who knew all the Burns and Allen routines. Now don't ask me how, because I don't remember them—but she knew them. I'd like you to meet her now. Ladies and gentlemen . . . Miss Lisa Miller.

(Lisa comes out)

Lisa, say hello.

LISA

Hello.

GEORGE

You see, it isn't easy to get laughs. Did you have a good time working in Vegas?

LISA

Oh yes. But I forgot to tell you what happened when I was there. I was standing next to this strange man at the dice table, and when he got through shooting he took me out and the next day he bought me a fur coat.

GEORGE

Bought you a fur coat?

LISA

A mink.

GEORGE

What did you have to do for it?

LISA

Just shorten the sleeves.

GEORGE

Now you *know* that she knows all the old Burns and Allen routines. . . . Lisa, which routine would you like to do tonight?

LISA

Well, there's the one about riding on the bus . . . or the backyard circus . . . or about Aunt Clara . . . or . . .

GEORGE

Let's do the one about riding on the bus.

LISA

I liked Aunt Clara. She had her own recipe for cooking roast beef. You take two roasts . . . a big one and a little one. You put them both in the oven, and when the little one burns, the big one is done.

GEORGE

I don't think I remember that one.

LISA

Sure you do. Remember one time when Aunt Clara woke up in the middle of the night and let out this big scream, and we all ran into her room and her feet had turned black?

GEORGE

What'd you do?

LISA

We sent for a doctor.

GEORGE

What did the doctor do?

LISA

He took off her stockings and we all went back to sleep again.

GEORGE

I don't know how, but I think I forgot that. . . . Let's do the bus routine.

LISA

I loved Aunt Clara. How about the time she stayed home one night because the canary was hatching an ostrich egg?

GEORGE

A canary was hatching an ostrich egg?

LISA

Yes, and the canary was too small to cover the egg.

GEORGE

So?

LISA

So Aunt Clara sat on the egg and held the canary in her lap.

GEORGE

Lisa . . .

LISA

Oh, all right. . . . So the other day I was riding on a bus.

"The Bus" then offered another two minutes of entertainment. This material always worked for the two of us, but in retrospect I understand that it would have

*At the Palmer House in Chicago,
before the new hairdo.*

worked for anyone because it was so perfectly constructed. GB eventually turned it into a three-way routine that we'd do with whomever else we shared the bill. In the meantime, we worked as "a single" for the next couple of engagements.

It was a few months after this show that GB and I went to play the Palmer House in Chicago in February of 1968.

GB would have done anything I wanted to make me happy, but what he didn't understand was that all I really wanted was to be with him. For this engagement, so that I wouldn't be lonely, he hired the Kids Next Door as the opening act. He still didn't realize that there was envy in the air, and I really didn't either. I just knew that I wasn't included in very many of their activities during the day, and was left to my own devices to keep myself amused.

One of the activities I chose turned out to be a rather poor choice. I went to the hair salon in the hotel and got a very tight permanent in my very short blond hair. I looked as if I'd slept with a French poodle. GB tried to be nice about it, but when I walked on stage that night it wasn't at all to his liking.

For the rest of the engagement, whenever we would sit on the sofa and watch TV in our suite, he'd reach over and touch my hair gently while sort of tugging at it. The tugging would eventually increase in intensity until he was actually pulling my hair! One night, I finally asked him what he thought he was doing. He got the "glint" and looked me right in the eyes and explained that he was trying to straighten out my tight little curls!

Then he angrily complained, "You never have time to rehearse but you always have time to do other things. I can't believe that you don't like to rehearse."

Knowing just what would get me in trouble, I answered back instead of just letting it go. "GB, you and I don't see it the same way. Let me ask you something."

The "glint" appeared as he waited for me to say something he would think of as "jerky."

"G'head."

"Has there ever been a time when we've worked together that any reviews said anything but good stuff about us working together and how I can hold my own with you on stage?"

"That's not the point!"

"You're right, that's *not* the point. You know I love show business but I always love being with you more. Being on stage is just a way to be with you!"

He looked at me expectantly to see what other stuff I'd say to try to defuse the argument. I knew what to say, so I continued, "I've *always* had the best time when we were working on the road."

"Why, if you don't like performing?"

He knew the answer. He'd heard it before.

"Because it's just us in the hotel."

Even though he'd heard all this many times before, he settled in to hear it again.

I always loved when we traveled because that was the only time we shared a bedroom and bathroom, unlike at home where he had his room and I had mine and what transpired between us was kept very private because he was a very private man with an effortless sense of propriety. But when we traveled, even though GB always booked a suite with two bedrooms, two bathrooms, and a sitting room, we were inseparable. I suppose we spent years of going through the charade of separate rooms for appearances' sake, but I'm still not quite sure for *whose* because it was never discussed—ever.

That's why being out of town was always the most fun. It was just us. I wore his pajama tops and he wore the bottoms. I'd watch while he, as he put it, would "run the razor" over his face after breakfast and then again, later that evening, before we'd go on stage.

I'd tease him as he'd carefully put his toupee on its block. After gently securing it to the block with straight pins, he'd turn to me as I stood lovingly watching and say, "Kid, the block looks great and I look like an old Jew!" Well, not to me he didn't. But, then again, what did I know? I'm an Episcopalian. I think he had what's commonly know as male-pattern baldness: early hair loss but, in his case, plenty of "fur" from the neck down and covering a truly well-kept body. Hardly an old man—at least never, ever in my eyes.

I loved watching GB prepare to go on stage with his elegant, crisp dress shirt and tie and cat's eye cuff buttons (which matched the ring Gracie had given him), garters and socks (this was a long time ago!), and always-ironed

Working together as a "single."

boxer shorts. (Years later I introduced him to the wonderful world of jockey shorts—we never made it to men's bikinis but I'm sure he'd have loved them even more than the jockeys!) He'd put everything on *but* his trousers, so over all of this, he always wore a beautiful silk dressing gown.

There he would be, with those wonderful straight, trim dancer's legs of his, only exposed from the knees down, extending beyond the hem of the dressing gown.

Men can be so different with everything on but their trousers. Some look silly.

Some pathetic. Then there are those who look especially powerful and seductive. It has nothing to do with stature and everything to do with a presence. There's something especially attractive about a man maintaining his sense of dignity and power and yet being pretty basically vulnerable to all sorts of dangers without pants on.

When on the road, my favorite event was having room-service meals together in *our* room. When the waiter knocked at the door I'd scurry into my bedroom to cringe. After our meal was set up and everything had been made ready, GB would call to me to come out. In the meantime, I'd go muss up the bed in my room so the maid wouldn't think that we'd been sharing his bed. Who *were* we kidding?

When I finished my confession about life on the road, which was (for me) a declaration of undying enchantment and love, I waited for GB's response. He hesitated a moment, then shook his head and said, "Kid, this may all be true and you know I love you, but you drive me out of my skull even though you're a darling girl."

"Okay, okay. Let's go over the routine if you want."

He'd always get in the last zinger. "Think you can still remember it?"

"I can if you can—since the last time we did it was about two hours ago on stage!"

GEORGE

Lisa . . .

LISA

Oh, all right. . . . So the other day I was riding on a bus.

GEORGE

That's better. Now, Lisa, why were you on a bus?

LISA

Because my car was in the shop.

GEORGE

What's wrong with it?

LISA

The same old thing. I've had nothing but trouble with
that car. Every time I hit something it puts a dent in it!

GEORGE

Well, I'd trade it in, if I were you.

LISA

That's what my boyfriend Feffering said when he took
it to the shop.

GEORGE

Wait a minute. You have a boyfriend and his name
is Feffering?

LISA

His father gave him that name, and it wasn't easy

to do because his father died before Feffering was born.

GEORGE

Then how was it possible for his father to give him that name?

LISA

He left a note to his mother.

GEORGE

If it wasn't for that note, his name might have been Charlie.

LISA

Feffering's father was from Texas. He was a very, very rich man.

GEORGE

Did he leave a will?

LISA

Oh yes, and when the lawyer read it to his married children it said that for each new child they had they'd get an extra hundred thousand dollars. But they weren't interested.

GEORGE

Weren't interested?

LISA

No. Before the lawyer could even finish the sentence the room was empty.

GEORGE

They were probably double-parked. . . . Now Lisa, let's get back to the bus.

LISA

All right. So I took this bus and this lady sat down next to me, and she asked me the silliest question you ever heard. She said, "Can I take this bus to the Plaza Hotel?"

GEORGE

What's silly about that?

LISA

You know the Plaza Hotel. They won't even let you take a dog in there.

GEORGE

Did you tell that to the lady?

LISA

Of course.

GEORGE

What did the lady say?

LISA

She didn't say anything, she just got up and moved to another seat.

GEORGE

Well, some people just don't appreciate good advice.

LISA

And then there are others who don't.

GEORGE

Well, that's another way to look at it. What happened next?

LISA

This man sat down next to me and he was working a crossword puzzle. We got to talking, and he told me he was an obstetrician and that last year he had 206 babies.

GEORGE

And what did you have to say about that?

LISA

I said to him, "I'll bet your wife doesn't have time to work crossword puzzles."

GEORGE

Lisa, an obstetrician is a doctor. He's the kind of a doctor that . . .

LISA

(Interrupting) Well, he certainly must be neglecting his practice if he's having all those babies.

GEORGE

Probably ruining his golf game, too. Did you have any more conversations with the doctor?

LISA

I was going to, but he moved, too.

GEORGE

I figured he would.

LISA

Then this girl who sat beside me wanted to know how to get to Main Street.

GEORGE

What did you say?

LISA

I told her just to watch where I got off and for her to get off eight blocks before I did.

GEORGE

And she moved, too.

LISA

No, I did.

GEORGE

You moved?

LISA

I figured everybody else was moving . . . why not?

GEORGE

Sounds like a pretty busy bus.

LISA

I took the seat right in back of the driver.

GEORGE

I suppose you and the driver had a little conversation.

LISA

Oh yes, he talked my ear off.

GEORGE

Like what?

LISA

Like telling me about the problem he's having with his two-year-old son. It seems that his little boy can't hold onto his food.

GEORGE

So?

LISA

So I told him for dinner to give the little boy a live lobster.

GEORGE

A live lobster?

> LISA
>
> If he can't hold onto his food
>
> GEORGE & LISA
>
> . . . he should have food that can hold onto him.
>
> LISA
>
> Yeah.
>
> GEORGE
>
> What did the driver think about that?
>
> LISA
>
> You'll never believe this, but it was the first time *I*
> ever drove a bus.

When we finished, GB looked at me for a minute and finally asked, "Kid, is that the end of the routine?"

With a very straight face, I replied, "Unless you want to hear some more about Aunt Clara."

We both started laughing, knowing that these two lines were *really* the end of the routine. Then he gave it one last try: "Kid, you're getting some good reviews here in Chicago, so why do you need to go home and go right back to college?"

"GB, you know I've always liked school."

"Yeah, well I like kosher hot dogs too, but that doesn't mean I want to eat them every day!"

How can you argue with that?

When we returned to Los Angeles, I moved into GB's house full time. UCLA was only ten minutes away, so I enrolled in a couple of classes.

GB was always supportive of my desire to go to school, although at times I know he just didn't understand it. His education stopped sometime around the fourth grade. Besides, despite my love of show business and the lore and a good "buck and wing," I didn't have the same drive as GB.

Once, when I was at UCLA, I told him I couldn't go on the road right then because I was taking finals. He wasn't so nice about it. We were walking up the stairs; he was ahead of me. I could tell by the way he was walking that he was getting angrier and angrier with my inflexibility. I pleaded with him, "GB, I've absolutely got to take a physics final. If I miss it I could get an incomplete or maybe even get an F!"

I was right behind him but when he got to the landing he stopped abruptly and turned to me. "Is taking a physics final anything like taking an enema?" That was GB's idea of being mean but I just started laughing, which made him even angrier.

·THREE·

*"Kid, I'm too old a cat to get taken
by a kitty like you!"*

In the spring of 1968, when I started living at GB's and going to school, I realized something was missing. Pets! We had no animals in the house and I missed it. My old cat Ting-A-Ling—see GB's book *Living It Up (Or, They Still Love Me in Altoona)* in which he talks about my cat—and my collie Fanny had gone to live with my parents when my mother remarried. Growing up I'd had cats, dogs, birds, and mice and was used to having some sort of animal life around the house. GB wasn't, but that still didn't deter me from starting the pet cavalcade that lasted until the end of GB's life. At one point, I even gave him a live bunny for Easter.

I'd gone skiing during spring break and came home the night before Easter. The next morning I presented him with a beautifully wrapped box while he was sitting at the breakfast table. He carefully untied the bow, of course not knowing what to expect, and then this bunny leaped out onto the breakfast table. And to complete the picture, it started eating his cereal!

GB was so surprised and tickled that morning. He immediately named the young rabbit Bunnikins. But it had taken me a whole year to work up to getting that rabbit. I knew that he'd had dogs when Gracie was alive and so dogs were where I had started the year before with the animal acquisitions.

I just went out one day during that first spring of 1968 when I had first started living at his house, and bought a dog. Not just any dog, but an apricot-colored toy poodle. With this on the heels of my beauty-shop escapade in Chicago, it meant that the dog and I had the same hair. Of course, GB was the first to point this out. Then when I took the dog out with me, everyone we ever ran into pointed that out. I named her Prunella the Jazz Baby but we called her Prunsie. I think the "prunes" part should have been a warning. The housebreaking was never successful, although GB tried and tried and was very diligent.

Every morning he would come into my room and, while I pretended I was asleep, he would gently remove Prunsie from my bed and take her downstairs. Then I would hear him outside trying to coax her to do her "stuff."

I heard him say, "Come on, Prunsie, do your stuff. You know you can boo-boo." And she always would—as soon as she came back into the house.

It didn't take long for this to wear thin, and I flew Prunella up to my mother's house for Mother's Day. My mother loved and pampered that awful dog for over ten years.

Next we moved on to kitties. I've always loved cats, so this one was easy. GB had never had a cat in his life until we started living together. Ben Cohn, who worked for GB, recommended a breed of cat called a Himalayan, which looks like a Siamese with Persian fur. I bought GB a pair of Himalayan kittens for Christmas 1968.

These first two kitties were Eli and Ramona. Ramona. Doesn't the name just roll off the tongue? I named her. GB loved her almost as much as he loves hot soup. Unfor-

tunately, Ramona had the mentality of a four-month-old kitten all of her life. For years, Ramona hardly ever went outside because she didn't understand what "outside" was. There was this one day good ol' Ramona was outside playing with her boyfriend Eli. (GB named him.) The cats were chasing each other round and round the pool while GB went up and down doing *his* poolside morning exercises.

Eventually, Eli put the pool between Ramona and himself. Ramona, perceptive kitty that she was, took the shortest route possible to catch Eli—across the pool.

Suddenly, she was airborne in a stretched-out Super Kitty pose minus the cape. We watched her sail about a third of the way across the pool and suddenly drop like a rock into the deep end, and continue "rocklike" straight to the bottom!

Although GB had on his bathing suit and I had on my pajamas, he designated me "kitty lifeguard." Afterward, as I was drying Ramona off with *his towel*, I said very seriously and thoughtfully, "Maybe Ramona really doesn't understand the concept of water."

GB replied without cracking a smile, "Maybe she needs glasses, Kid."

I didn't think it was very funny at the time and responded, "Or maybe she knows what water is and thinks she can walk on it." Big pause and I continued, "Just like some other people we know but I won't mention any names."

He didn't answer me with that one so I gave it one more shot.

"GB, you must admit there is something not quite right when a person in a bathing suit makes a person who's not in a bathing suit jump into a swimming pool to rescue a cat that probably could have rescued herself."

"Kid, Ramona is not the kind of kitty who could have rescued herself."

GB has always referred to all of the various cats as "the kitties" and it always made me smile.

During the following year, which included the addition of Bunnikins, we sadly had to have Eli put down due to kidney failure. But GB still had Ramona and they continued having this mad, passionate kitty love affair. She would lie on the breakfast table by his elbow while he ate his breakfast and read the paper. At dinner GB would have the help give him a little dish and he would cut up bits of his dinner for her to eat. When he went up to bed at night, she would always beat him there and be waiting for him on his bed. He really did turn out to be a true cat person.

·FOUR·

*"Kid, now that you're back in college
I want you to answer something for
me. If a man limps on both legs, does
he limp?"*

Between going to college, managing the "pet brigade," rehearsing, and working, GB and I settled into a regular sort of semi-matrimonial, suburban rhythm. Well, that may be simplifying things a bit.

While we'd been performing at the Palmer House, Neil Bogart, then at Buddah Records, flew in to see the show and visit with GB about the possibility of making an album. GB was *very* excited and he asked me to sit in on the meeting. By the end of that session it was a go-ahead.

When we got back to Los Angeles the record company sent their choice of record producer and an arranger/conductor, Larry Fallon, who went on to work as GB's conductor for years. They discussed material, and GB, of course, wanted to do the medley that he'd done with the Kids Next Door in Vegas and Chicago. Then he asked me about some music. At that time, I was listening to Harry Nilsson, the Beatles, the Rolling Stones, and the Brandenburg Concertos. He passed on the Brandenburgs for obvious reasons. But he did end up using songs I suggested from the other groups.

When it came time to organize the recording dates, GB told me he wanted me to sing backup. I wasn't so sure about it. He insisted on it because I could sing harmony, which may have been true—I can sing and I have formally studied voice, both popular and classical—but that doesn't mean I'm a great singer. Sometimes I occasionally hit some good notes, and if they're not good then they're at least interesting. But . . . backup???

Larry Fallon then asked me if I could contract the backup vocalists for the album. I hired any of the Kids Next Door I could find. And the recording sessions were hilarious!

GB loved singing so much and was so funny in the studio. He drove the musicians and engineers crazy, but those of us singing with him had worked with him before so we were nonplussed by it all.

Right after this, we celebrated our second Fourth of July (the first being the year before when we'd first come back to Los Angeles from Vegas).

This second one was a real doozy.

One night early in that summer, GB and I saw an ad on TV for fireworks being sold somewhere near Inglewood. Right then and there we decided that it would be fun to buy some and to order cracked crab and Nova Scotia salmon from Hillcrest and have some fun at home for the Fourth.

I wrote down the address of the fireworks place and the next evening after dinner GB and I got in the car and headed there. We found this huge stand in the middle of nowhere with a towering RED DEVIL FIREWORKS sign. This was it. We parked the car in the dirt lot and started over to the displays. Of course, I'd forgotten I was with a celebrity—not just my GB. No one came over to us but our presence certainly did create a stir.

We checked out all the different combinations of fireworks. GB pulled out his money clip and bought the biggest assortment available.

Boy, were we going to have some fun! We invited my brother Graham, who was nervously preparing to get married that August, to come for dinner that night. I also invited my girlfriend, Susan Somerville, to come for the entire long weekend.

Right after dinner, the four of us went into the backyard. GB sat down to smoke a cigar (that seemed a little redundant considering what we had in front of us!) and the three of us started setting things up for our private show.

Styrofoam pool floats with roman candles on them, oranges in the orange trees studded with pinwheels, sparklers in the flower pots. With everything all set up, we raced around the yard igniting everything. And that's just what happened. Everything ignited!

The pool floats took off and the roman candles immediately fell in the water but instead of being doused, because they have the same ingredients as a flare, they continued to burn and spin around in the water. The pinwheels in the orange trees became projectiles when lit and ripped the oranges out of the trees and continued to fly around the yard like miniature grenades. The sparklers didn't do the geraniums any good, either.

The three of us were stupefied, which isn't surprising considering the stupidity of what we'd done. As the yard filled with smoke and the scent of gunpowder, GB sat enjoying his cigar and watching the show as if it were all going exactly as we had intended. At least until the smoke cleared. Then we had a good look at things.

The inside of the pool was scorched. There were smoldering oranges randomly lying around the yard, and the pots of geraniums had been reduced to smudge pots.

Graham had gotten the hose and was saturating anything that still looked "live." I ran over to GB and started profusely apologizing.

"Nice work, Kid. Leave it to you. Now, why don't you kids finish tidying up and we'll go in the house and have some cookies and ice cream."

That was it. No recriminations. No chastisement.

I remember that after Graham left, GB said that he hoped Graham's wedding wouldn't be quite so loud and that his wedding night would be a little more under control than the hose he'd just been using in the backyard. Susan turned bright red but by now I was shocked by very few of GB's jokes and was actually getting good at an occasional contribution of my own.

GB wasn't so far wrong about Graham's wedding that August. The wedding night I don't know anything about.

Graham and his fiancée were married in a very elaborate wedding that her parents had carefully orchestrated. But that didn't stop GB and the Miller family from placing their own stamp on the occasion.

After the ceremony when we arrived at the reception at the local country club, GB got any of my family he could into the bar. Once there, he held court for the entire evening. As a bridesmaid, I was required to be other places, but every time I returned to the bar he was up to mischief. First of all he got my mother and Lee there for a few cocktails. Then he had someone go and get my "biological" father who was there with his "other wife and daughter."

With all of them in the same jurisdiction and under the influence of a few martinis, GB tried to get my parents to reconcile! This kind of behavior went on for hours until they closed the bar on us.

Next we all went back into Beverly Hills to a deli that no longer exists called Lenny's. It was the only place still open. Once there, we all ate up a storm as GB did his shtick, which never fails to make me laugh.

At one point, he put his hand under the table and knocked underneath it. My family all looked at him expectantly, waiting for our usual "knock-knock" jokes. He looked at me and I gave him the look back, waiting. I knew what he was going to say and he did.

"Oh, pardon me," he grinned. I interrupted to inform everyone, "That was his *dickie*." With that he turned to me and corrected, "That's *Mr. Dickie* to you!"

From there he went into a series of "dickie" jokes that had my family falling on the floor until the management finally begged us to let them close the restaurant.

A few days after the wedding I went up north for a visit to my mother and Lee's. When I returned it was back to school and *work* (read *rehearsal*—my nemesis).

We were booked on a Bob Hope show and it was the first time we'd ever tried the act as a three-way rather than a two-way routine.

It didn't make any difference to me. Whoever was the straight man got the same answers! All I had to do was answer the person who asked me the questions.

During The Bob Hope Show.

SEPTEMBER 1968
HOPE-MILLER-BURNS

GEORGE
Lisa, this is Bob Hope.

LISA
Hello, Mr. Hope.

BOB
Hello, Lisa.

LISA
Oh, I'm so happy to meet you, Mr. Hope. And I must

tell you, you look much younger since you shaved off your beard.

                    BOB

I never had a beard.

                    LISA

Well, that would be impossible. Then how could you shave it off?

                    BOB

I didn't shave it off.

                    LISA

Well, whoever did, did you a favor. You look much better without it.

                    BOB

George, if these are the right answers, I must be asking some pretty stupid questions.

                   GEORGE

Lisa, I don't think Mr. Hope understands you.

                    LISA

Oh? Mr. Hope, would you like me to talk slower?

BOB

Oh no, no, I'll just try to listen faster.

LISA

Well, whatever makes you comfortable. You know, I watch you all the time on TV, and I love the finish of your show where you always smile at the audience and wave your hand and say, "God bless."

BOB

Lisa, Red Skelton does that.

LISA

Well, he should be ashamed of himself. Now you'll have to get a new finish.

BOB

George, you better take over while I let my beard grow.

GEORGE

All right. Lisa, did anything exciting happen today?

GEORGE

(Before she can answer—to Bob) Bob, would you care to jump in again?

BOB

I'm not dried off from the last time.

GEORGE

Well, Bob, just ask her if anything interesting happened to her on the bus coming over here.

BOB

That sounds safe enough. Lisa, did anything interesting happen to you on the bus coming over here?

LISA

Absolutely nothing.

BOB

Good.

LISA

Except for one thing.

BOB

I'm back in again.

And we were back in the bus routine that was to remain one of the mainstays of
all the routines we did together for the next six months.

Of course, there were always minor changes. GB was always "improving" the bit and then wanting to rehearse. I think the only time we didn't fight about rehearsing was when I worked on GB's record. To me, that wasn't rehearsing—it was "practicing." I'd done that for years when I studied piano.

The next time we worked was a Gleason show in Miami. We did the same routine, so there didn't seem to be any great need to rehearse and we had time off. I decided that since we had a couple of days off, I'd make a fast day trip to Nassau. Don't ask why. I don't know myself. GB didn't want to go so I asked his conductor, Larry Fallon, to go with me. And we went. All I really remember is that I got a truly horrible sunburn in that one day. And GB was furious with me. It was years before I realized that he wasn't mad about the painful sunburn; he was mad that I went off for the day without him and *with* another man. Talk about stupid. It was twenty years before I'd realized that he'd been jealous! What he didn't realize was that it never dawned on me to cheat on him while we were together. He was all I wanted.

When we taped the show, it was necessary to give me some serious body makeup because I looked like a lobster. Of course, the routine had been adapted somewhat to fit the *Jackie Gleason Show* framework.

10/11/68
BURNS-GLEASON-MILLER

(AFTER JACKIE INTRODUCES GEORGE)

JACKIE
Incidentally, George, who's that young girl backstage
that you brought with you from California?

GEORGE

Her name is Lisa Miller, and she worked with me in Las Vegas. She was with an act called the Kids Next Door, and she knows all the old Burns and Allen routines. How she remembers them I'll never know, because I don't.

JACKIE

I'd *love* to hear you do one of those routines.

GEORGE

Why don't you do it with me?

JACKIE

George, to do a routine like that you've got to be a real straight man. I don't think I could do it.

GEORGE

Jackie, it's simple, and there's no pressure on you. You don't have to worry about getting any laughs.

JACKIE

Hmmm, maybe I've been a straight man all these years and didn't know it.

GEORGE

Well, I'll bring her out and we'll split her between us.

Ladies and gentlemen, Miss Lisa Miller.

(Lisa comes out)

Lisa, this is Jackie Gleason.

JACKIE

Hello, Lisa.

LISA

Hello, Mr. Gleason. When my mother heard I was going to be on your show she was thrilled. She told me to tell you that you're her favorite comedian.

JACKIE

Thank you. You must have a very nice mother.

LISA

Oh yes, we treat her like one of the family.

GEORGE

Well, that's because her family is very close.

LISA

But, Mr. Gleason, you're my favorite, too—that is, you and Willard Newton.

JACKIE

Who's Willard Newton?

LISA

He's a boy in my biology class. I told him I'd mention
his name.

GEORGE

Well, Jackie, now you know why she remembers all
the Burns and Allen routines. Well, Lisa, which one
of the routines would you like to do?

And then, of course, we went right into the bus routine.

We flew back from Miami the day of my twentieth birthday, and there was dinner
at the house with my whole family. Two months later, we celebrated Christmas at
GB's house, once again with the entire family.

Christmas. Ever since I was a little girl it's been my least favorite holiday. As a
child it always seemed to create so much pressure, which resulted in everyone being
short-tempered and more concerned with what had to be bought for people and
where the money was to come from rather than the true meaning of the season. Luckily, GB felt as I did.

He said right up front that he didn't believe in buying a lot of gifts for people he
didn't care about just because it was Christmas. He thought that if you felt like giving someone a gift you should do it whenever you felt like it. Our first Christmas

together, he gave me a beautiful pale pink suede shirt-dress and I gave him a case of ketchup. It was the only thing he liked that I could afford! He was really tickled and never failed to mention it every Christmas thereafter.

Our second Christmas, after we returned from Miami, turned out to be a real family affair.

My mother and Lee came down from Northern California for one week. On Christmas morning, they came over with Graham and his "bridelet." GB and I cooked *them* Christmas breakfast.

He said he'd make his special "cottage fried potatoes" since it was the help's day off. The potatoes this Christmas morning were truly special for, of course, more reasons than one. This is his recipe on the opposite page. (He claimed his secret was using half butter and half oil so that the grease wouldn't burn.)

GB making his famous cottage fries.

New Year's seemed to come so quickly that year. GB flew to Vegas early for New Year's, and I was to join him a couple of days later. But while I was staying at the house alone, something very frightening happened that ended up being all for the best but took awhile to straighten itself out.

The people who worked for GB at the time (and shall remain nameless because

GB's Special Cottage Fried Potatoes

4 large baking potatoes
4 tbsp. unsalted butter
4 tbsp. vegetable oil
salt and pepper

Scrub the potatoes and slice VERY thin. As you slice them drop them in water that has ice cubes in it.

After slicing the potatoes put the butter and the oil in an iron skillet and heat slowly so the mixture doesn't burn.

While this is heating, remove the potatoes from the water and dry EACH slice thoroughly.

Very carefully put one slice at a time in the hot butter and oil until there is a layer of potatoes at the bottom of the skillet. Turn each potato slice individually until crispy. Remove to a layer of paper towel and lightly salt, put another layer of paper towel on top, and once again place a layer of potatoes at the bottom of the skillet. Continue in this same manner until all the potatoes are cooked!

P.S. Keep the plate with the cooked potatoes in a very low oven to keep them warm because cooking potatoes like this "could kill a season in show business," as GB repeatedly told me while he was cooking.

I'm still afraid of them) decided after GB left for Vegas that it was time to get rid of me.

This same couple had been let go earlier in the year for some serious grocery bill padding. And I must admit that I instigated the dismissal. But when we couldn't find suitable replacements, GB got them to come back. Now, whenever GB wasn't looking, they gave me a seriously hard time, and this was certainly no exception.

I'd come home this one afternoon and gone directly up to my bedroom. The butler and his oafish son (who looked and acted like Lenny from *Of Mice and Men*) were shooting pool in the billiard room right off my bedroom.

I very politely asked them if they could please leave since I had things to do in my room and knew that they shouldn't have been there anyway. They just laughed at me. So I just shrugged and walked toward the police buzzer. With that, the butler sneered at me, "By the time they get here, they won't be able to help you!"

With my heart pounding, I answered, "By the time I get back from Vegas *no one* will be able to help you!"

I beat a hasty retreat, got in my car, and drove myself to the airport with nothing but the clothes on my back.

By the time I arrived in Vegas I was a wreck. I found GB in our suite at the hotel, breathlessly told him what had happened, and then started to cry and carry on that they were so evil and dishonest that they'd probably hurt the kitties while we were gone, and so on.

GB went in the next room, made a couple of phone calls, and came back to me. He told me to get something to wear for that night and go wash my face. I didn't ask him what he had done because I didn't want to know, but when we flew home the next day, just as we arrived at LAX, he turned to me, held my hand, and said, "Kid, I want you to get your car and keep yourself busy for a couple of hours. When you come home, they'll be gone."

And they were. There was just one hitch: Once again there was no one to run the house.

·FIVE·

"You make a mistake once, that's honest. You make the same mistake twice, you're stupid!"

For the next two months I cleaned GB's great big house, did the marketing and cooking, made the beds, and with the help of a lady who came once a week, did our laundry. I had been cleaning house at my mother's, which included polishing silver, doing the laundry, and my ironing, since I was in the fifth grade. GB's window sills were never so clean as when I would do them during this time! I'd also learned my way around a kitchen at an early age, so that part of this new role wasn't too difficult— especially since GB didn't care what he ate as long as it was hot. In fact, taking care of him with just the two of us in the house was really fun. He seemed to appreciate everything that I did for him.

Well, there was one exception. Dinner. I always thought the hot soup we ate needed to be started with a homemade stock, so I spent hours preparing stock as the base for my soups. One afternoon, GB came home and found me in the kitchen futzing with the soup. He asked me what I was doing and I told him.

"Kid, listen to me. Campbell's pays their chefs big bucks to come up with all their soups. Just do like all the cooks in this house have done, and start with a can of their soup and augment it!"

He did have to teach me how to make matzo, eggs, and onions. It was one of our favorite dinners, along with kosher hot dogs and new pickles from Hillcrest. When I've shared this recipe people have looked at me as if I had two heads, but here's how GB taught me to make it (see facing page).

We finally hired a new couple but we should have known right away that it wasn't going to work. They were named Ken and, of all things, Gracie.

The first indication that things might not work out was the fact that "she" couldn't get the hang of matzo, eggs, and onions. Finally, GB and I took them to Hillcrest for lunch so she could taste it firsthand. She not only ate matzo, eggs, and onions but also drank her weight in gin flips and proceeded to get completely looped at lunch.

GB was so desperate to have someone other than yours truly running the house that he went out of his way to make their working conditions ideal. One of the perks was that they could use the swimming pool. Unfortunately, she always chose to use the pool when we were out there, *and* she'd put on a water ballet and become a one-person synchronized swim team. But what really did it was the outfit she wore out to the pool.

GB's Matzo, Eggs, and Onions
(obviously only for TWO)

4 eggs
1 small onion

1 full sheet of Matzo
ice water

Sauté the chopped onion in a bit of oil or butter until it's transparent.

In the meantime, beat the eggs with a couple of tablespoons of ice water. Sprinkle the sheet of matzo with some of the ice water so it is PLIABLE BUT NOT SOAKED!

Now, here's the tricky part. Break up the dampened matzo into bit-sized pieces and add it to the beaten eggs. Combine briefly--you must hurry!

Now pour the eggs and matzo into the skillet with the onions. Quickly, and gently, toss them together and then leave them alone!

That's it. At least for us it always was.

She'd come out in a trench coat and rubber shoes, stop dramatically at the far end of the pool, and wait to see if we were watching. After a dramatic pause, she'd gracefully drop her coat, do a swan dive into the pool, and go into her water ballet routine.

It wasn't working with them. It just wasn't working at all. And as time went on things got "curiouser and curiouser." She kept insisting to GB and me that her "poor Ken" wasn't quite himself but that he was a good man and she'd make sure that he stayed under control. She alluded to the fact that he had manic-depressive potential after having been a London bobby for many years. He certainly did have a distinctive way of walking, if that was any indication. In fact, it was so distinctive that GB and I couldn't get away from it. No matter where this man went in the house and no matter what kind of flooring he was walking on, you could definitely hear him. With every step he took, you could hear him first set down his heel with a definite thud and then proceed to put down the rest of his foot. Heel, toe, heel, toe. It started driving GB absolutely nuts! So GB paid for this man to have all the leather heels of his shoes replaced with rubber in order to try and muffle the sound. And it didn't.

During this shoe episode (which lasted several weeks), we had a minor earthquake one night during dinner. As GB and I sat watching the water slosh in the swimming pool, "she" came rushing in while struggling to get into her trench coat and babbling something about the air raids in London during World War II. I think that was when GB and I realized that Ken wasn't the one with the problem. The only problem he had was his loony wife!

This eccentric behavior continued but we didn't know what to do because having them in the house was still better than not having anyone—even if she couldn't cook, he couldn't walk, and they both despised the cats!

It was during this time that something happened with GB that made me realize he was really getting frazzled and addlepated by this whole experience. My girlfriend and I had gone to see a play at UCLA and it ended up being much longer than we thought. Because it was so late when she dropped me off at GB's, I told her she should sleep over rather than return to the dorm.

Very quietly we came in. I didn't go into GB's room to tell him we were home because I knew he'd been asleep for hours, so we just got into bed. Just as we were almost asleep, I saw the door of my bedroom slowly open and as I got ready to push the police alarm at my bedside, I saw that the silhouette was GB's. He looked directly at the bed, and from the light behind him in the hall I could see that he looked terribly worried. But since he was staring right at me without saying anything, I remained silent, too.

After looking around my room, he went to my desk and sat down. By now we were all awake, but still none of us had said anything. Then GB turned on my desk light. I figured he wasn't playing with a full deck anymore and I had better let him do whatever it was that he was going to do.

He picked up the phone. Then it hit me. He was looking for me and he was going to call around and find out where I was! He had been in my room all this time but he hadn't seen us in bed watching him. Unbelievable but true!

He looked so funny but also very worried and unsure of what he was going to do. I knew that if we said "Hello," he'd jump out of his skin, and that if he called my friend's house and there was no answer (and there wouldn't be since we were both lying in bed watching him), we'd be in big trouble for staying out so late. Then, just as he started to dial the phone, a small giggle escaped from one of us. GB looked up, checked out the room again, but *still* didn't see us and continued to dial the phone. Pretty goofy, huh?

Finally, we both laughed out loud. We always laughed a lot when we were around

GB, and that in turn used to make him laugh a lot so I guess we thought that laughing out loud might lighten up the situation. Well, it didn't.

GB looked at the bed and this time his eyes sort of screwed up and he got his famous "glint" in them. With that he put the phone down, closed my address book, turned off the light, and left without saying a word.

The odd part was that he never did admit it happened, and I began to fear that maybe he just didn't remember!

In a wonderful stroke of luck, Arlette and Daniel came to run the house for GB. From that moment on, until the end of his life, GB was taken care of by them in their own effortless, calm, and caring style. And I must say they certainly spoiled me over the years.

With the house back in order we were back on schedule: me going to school, GB going to the office and Hillcrest, and, whenever possible, GB trying to get me to rehearse.

During this time we were invited back to do a second Bob Hope show. I teased GB by telling him that even though I didn't like to rehearse, it couldn't have been *that* bad or they wouldn't have invited us back! He characteristically told me that I was never bad but I could have been better.

This is the Hope routine with the changes GB made for our second appearance.

SPRING 1969
HOPE-MILLER-BURNS

BOB

It amazes me to see a man your age with such a young body.

GEORGE

Well, thanks, Bob.

BOB

I saw her backstage. Who is she?

GEORGE

You remember her, she was on your show last year. Her name is Lisa Miller.

BOB

Oh yeah, she worked with you. That's the kid who's a little off-center. Is she still as flaky as ever?

GEORGE

No, she's changed completely. I was with her at a party the other night, and the hostess happened to mention she was fixing some lasagna with tomato paste. And Lisa said to her, "Why bother fixing it with tomato paste? If I had a broken lasagna, I'd throw it away."

BOB

George, I can't believe she said that.

GEORGE

Well, bring her out.

BOB

Okay. Lisa! Come on out!
(Enter Lisa)
Hello, Lisa.

LISA

Hello, Mr. Hope. I just love your TV show. I watch it
every week.

BOB

But I'm not on every week.

LISA

I'm such a big fan of yours that I watch you whether
you're on or not.

BOB

(To George) Now I believe the lasagna story.

GEORGE

I knew you would. (To Lisa) Lisa, you were a little late
getting here today.

LISA

Well, Mr. Burns, I never drove a bus before.

GEORGE

You drove a bus to get here?

LISA

I had to.

This is where we returned to the "bus routine" which continued pretty much the same as it had the first time we did it.

That summer we played Vegas and reverted the routine to its original two-person form, but it still had the same base: illogical logic with the same jokes reworked to perfection, but always with room for improvement. GB also added a song and a sand dance for us. This, of course, meant more rehearsing, but I always seemed to find some way to get out of it.

This was the first time we'd worked in Vegas since we'd met during my days with the Kids Next Door. During this engagement, we did the usual two shows a night at eight and midnight, but this time we worked thirty days straight without a break. I didn't know any better and thought everyone worked like that. But I did get numb after a while.

One night, I wandered on stage tardy for my intro and GB asked me in front of a thousand people if I needed a wake-up call for the next show. I was too stupid to even be embarrassed!

I must admit that I was slightly preoccupied toward the end of the engagement. Between shows, GB had introduced me to the pit boss of the casino and he in turn taught me how to shoot craps. I thought it was absolutely the best thing I'd ever learned except maybe for the prologue to *The Canterbury Tales* in Middle English. But GB made me promise that I would never go into the casino without him since I was underage. And by no stretch of the imagination was I ever to go to any of the gaming tables alone. I suppose it was a bit odd. I was in college during the school year and during the summer I was doing two shows a night in Vegas and "covering the hardway eight."

Seeing the Jack Benny show at the Sands.

Of course, I went into the casino and, of course, he caught me covering all the numbers and winning a bet on the "hardway eight." And boy, did I get into trouble. It seems like I was always getting in trouble for goofy stuff!

We returned to Los Angeles at the end of the summer just in time for me to start back to school. Not long after we got back, Dick Martin of the comedy team Rowan & Martin (who'd hosted *Laugh-In* in the late '60s) asked GB to try out a new project for him. It was to be a comedy beta cassette that would be available for home use. It seemed like an interesting concept so GB said yes and asked me if I wanted to work with him on it. Then to make his offer even more tantalizing, he told me we'd be doing a new routine. He'd tricked me! With new material, there was no way that rehearsing could be optional. But I really didn't mind this time because I loved the new routine.

It was taped in GB's living room and it was to seem that I was just coming home from school and into the room. Filming at the house was really fun. There were crews and cables all over and I ditched school for the day. This was the first time we incorporated "The Brothers Routine." Of course, GB also rewrote the opening of the routine to fit the situation.

CASSETTE 1969
BURNS-MILLER-MARTIN

GEORGE

(Looking off) Dick, there's Lisa pulling up in the driveway. Now Dick, before you meet her you ought to know one thing. She's got sort of an offbeat sense of humor. She makes sense, but the wrong kind of sense. You'll see what I mean. Lisa, come on in.

LISA

Hello, Mr. Burns.

GEORGE

Lisa Miller, this is Dick Martin.

DICK

Hello, Lisa. George tells me you might be good for my show.

LISA

I hope so, Mr. Martin, because I love your show. Especially the opening where you slide down that pole.

DICK

No, you're thinking of Dean Martin.

LISA

Oh, I like him, too. I like the finish of his show where he waves his fingers at the audience and says, "God Bless."

DICK

That's Red Skelton.

LISA

Really? Then who's Jackie Gleason?

DICK

Well, he's the one who's married to Mary Livingston.

LISA

Oh, that's where I got mixed up. I always thought she was married to Jack Benny.

GEORGE

No, no, he's the one who slides down the pole.

LISA

Oh well, that clears up the whole thing for me.

GEORGE

Well, Lisa, let's start The Brothers Routine.

LISA

Which brother do you want to talk about: the one who's married or the one who's in love?

GEORGE

Let's talk about the one who's in love.

LISA

Oh, that would be my brother Graham. You know, one time Graham fell down a flight of stairs with a bottle of gin and he never spilled a drop!

DICK

He never spilled a drop?

LISA

Of course not. He never opened his mouth!

GEORGE

You know, Dick, her brother Graham is with the FBI.

DICK

He is?

LISA

Oh, yeah. They picked him up in Kansas City.

DICK

Why did they pick him up?

LISA

Well, Kansas is a dry state.

DICK

And . . . ?

LISA

And Graham wasn't in a dry state!

GEORGE

So the FBI picked him up.

LISA

They had to—he couldn't pick himself up.

DICK

This kid sounds like one of my family.

GEORGE

You haven't heard anything. Graham once broke his back on account of a doughnut.

DICK

(To Lisa) A doughnut broke your brother's back?

LISA

Yeah, he loves doughnuts because he talks so much. He never stops talking.

DICK

George, what's talking got to do with it?

GEORGE

It's simple. With a doughnut he can eat and talk through the hole at the same time.

LISA

Of course. (Sotto, to George, about Dick) Is he all right?

GEORGE

(Sotto) I think so.

DICK

Now wait a minute. Lisa, how could a doughnut break your brother's back?

LISA

Well, Graham's left-handed.

DICK

(Long pause; then, puzzled) George, would you like to take the next line?

GEORGE

No. You started it. You finish it.

DICK

(To Lisa) Well, so your brother Graham is left-handed.

LISA

And he had a doughnut in his right-hand pocket, and he tried to get it out with his left hand and—he broke his back.

DICK

(Taking it away from her) . . . he broke his back.

LISA

Yeah.

GEORGE

You see, Dick, there's a reason that even though he had a doughnut in his right-hand pocket, he didn't take it out with his right hand.

LISA

Sure. That's very hard to do when you've got your pants on backwards.

DICK

He had his pants on backwards?

LISA

You see, Graham bought a suit with two pairs of pants, and he put one pair on frontwards and one pair on backwards.

GEORGE

That's so he could go either way.

LISA

That's when the truck hit him.

DICK

Truck! What truck?

LISA

The truck that didn't have its lights on.

DICK

Well, why didn't the man in the truck have his lights on?

LISA

He didn't have to—it was daytime.

DICK

If it was daytime, didn't the man in the truck see your brother coming?

LISA

He didn't know it was my brother.

GEORGE

How would he know? He never met the man.

LISA

That's right. He just saw two pairs of pants coming toward him . . . and he drove between them.

GEORGE & DICK

(Taking it away) . . . and he drove between them.

LISA

Yeah.

DICK

Lisa, be at the studio Monday morning at ten o'clock and we'll see about putting you on the show.

LISA

Oh, thank you, Mr. Martin. Good-bye.

DICK

Good-bye.

LISA

Good-bye, Mr. Burns.

GEORGE

Good-bye, Lisa.
(Lisa starts to exit, stops; then, to Dick)

LISA

Oh, Mr. Martin, when I get there Monday, can I slide
down your pole?

DICK

You certainly can.
(Lisa exits)

DICK

I can't believe it. Is she for real?

GEORGE

You caught her on one of her good days. Sometimes
she doesn't make any sense at all.

At the time I didn't realize the possible double entendre of the "sliding down the
pole" joke. I thought for years to come that it was a funny reference to the opening
of *The Dean Martin Show.* Oh well.

GB was suddenly starting to work all the time. It seemed that when we first met,
he never had as much work as he would have liked now that he was working a solo
act without Gracie. But after the record album and the TV appearances, there were
so many offers that GB definitely could pick and choose what he wanted to do.

He'd been asked to go to London for a TV show, and we both decided that it could
really be fun since he hadn't been out of the country in years and I hadn't *ever* been
out of the country.

The show was a variety show called *The Max Bygraves Show*. It was a sort of English take on a Dean Martin or Jackie Gleason show. We had the routine down pat, even though there had been a few changes, because, as GB explained to me, English audiences sometimes had a different sense of humor.

GB hadn't worked in England for years but he kept me thoroughly engrossed with the various stories about when he and Gracie first played there during the '30s and were a big hit doing the Lamb Chops routine. We planned to go and revisit some of the spots he loved.

That first trip to England was certainly one of the best times we ever had together.

We were met at the airport by the most beautiful car in the world—a Daimler. It looked like a Rolls Royce and a Bentley combined and had the most exotic hood ornament I've ever seen. From the airport we were driven to the Dorchester Hotel, where we were taken care of by dozens of people and shown to our suite. It was enchanting.

Our suite had a sitting room with wonderful frumpy chintz sofas by a funny sort of coal fireplace. On either end of the sitting room were our bedrooms. Each had its own huge tiled bathroom with heated towel racks. It was like being in a fairy tale.

We unpacked with assistance from the staff. Ladies took our clothes to have them pressed, which was very important to GB since he was always very meticulous about his appearance. I remember that he couldn't understand why I didn't want to send my clothes to be pressed, too. I kept insisting that it wasn't necessary and he kept firmly insisting, "You know, Kid, sometimes you're just too stubborn for your own good."

"GB, I'm sticking with it: Why get them pressed when they just get wrinkled again as soon as you put them on?"

I waited a beat and looked him right in the eye and continued, "Besides, I like wrinkles."

Without missing a beat, he replied, "Don't worry, I'll keep a wrinkle in it for you."

"Boy, I really set you up for that one."

"Yeah, well, it wasn't such a great setup."

"It wasn't meant to be a big joke."

"Are we still talking about the same thing?"

That first night we ate downstairs in the Dorchester's dining room. GB told me to put on "something nice" because we were going to have dinner downstairs in the "good dining room."

And it was the best. He ordered for me. By now I was fairly competent at ordering what I wanted but GB loved the fact that I would try anything. GB started eating Dover sole the very first meal there and it seemed like that was all he ordered for the next two weeks! We had a wonderful dinner, but the dessert was the best. We had tiny, perfect glacéed fruits that I still remember as being some of the most delicious things I've ever tasted.

The next day we went to rehearsal and met Mr. Bygraves, who couldn't have been nicer. Jim Backus was there and I knew him and his wife Henny from home. There was lots of laughing and Vaudeville and Palladium stories and funny acts that I'd never heard of. We ran through our routine as follows:

MAX BYGRAVES SHOW—12/69
BURNS-BYGRAVES-MILLER

MAX

George, who's that young girl backstage that you brought with you from America?

GEORGE

Her name is Lisa Miller, and she works with me in Las Vegas. She was with an act called the Kids Next Door, and she knows all the old Burns and Allen routines. How she remembers them I'll never know, because I don't.

MAX

I'd love to hear you do one of those routines.

GEORGE

Why don't you do it with me?

MAX

George, to do a routine like that you've got to be a real straight man. I don't think I could do it.

GEORGE

Max, it's simple, and there's no pressure on you. You don't have to worry about getting any laughs.

MAX

Hmmmm, maybe I've been a straight man all these years and didn't know it.

GEORGE

Well, I'll bring her out and we'll split her between us. Ladies and gentlemen, Miss Lisa Miller. Lisa, this is Max Bygraves.

MAX

Hello, Lisa.

LISA

Hello, Mr. Bygraves, and I'm so happy meet you. I watch your shows all the time, and I love them. In fact, everybody in America loves them.

MAX

But my show isn't seen in America.

LISA

I know. But my mother told me when I got to England I should be polite.

MAX

You must have a nice mother.

LISA

Oh, yes, she's like one of the family.

GEORGE

You know, Max, Lisa and her whole family, they all live together.

LISA

Oh yes. My brothers, my father, my uncle, my nephew—they all sleep in one bed.

MAX

I'm surprised your grandfather isn't sleeping with them.

LISA

Oh, he was. But he died so they made him get up.

GEORGE

Hm-m-m. Max, she comes from a very interesting family. She's got a brother with an appendicitis scar on his neck.

LISA

That's my brother Graham. And I have another brother, Philip, who sleeps on the floor, and my Aunt Clara . . .

GEORGE

Your brother Philip, why does he sleep on the floor?

LISA

Because he has high blood pressure.

GEORGE

And he's trying to keep it down?

LISA

Yeah.

MAX

Well, that explains Philip. But you say you've got a brother Graham who's got an appendicitis scar on his neck?

LISA

Oh, yeah, and even when he wears a high collar you can see it. The only time the scar doesn't show is when he takes his shoes off.

MAX

George, I don't understand that.

GEORGE

Well, you see, Max, when he takes his shoes off, his neck slips down into his collar.

MAX

That makes sense. But Lisa, why does he have the appendicitis scar on his neck?

LISA

(Pointing to her side) Well, he was so ticklish down here that they had to operate up here. (Pointing to her neck)

MAX

(Taking it away from her and pointing to his neck) . . . that they had to operate up here.

LISA

Yeah.

GEORGE

Now ask her about her aunt who had to stay home because her canary was hatching an ostrich egg.

MAX

George, I wouldn't ask her that for all the money in
the world.

GEORGE

Now that you know she knows all the Burns and Allen
routines. . .

From here we went into "The Brothers Routine" about Philip and Graham except
we left out the jokes about the FBI and Kansas. After all, we were in England and
we didn't know any jokes about Scotland Yard that we could use instead.

Everything was just perfect except for this comment from Mr. Bygraves at the end
of our first read-through.

"Lisa, if it's all right with you and Mr. Burns, I think we should work together
later on in the show. You did a fine job."

Well, it wasn't all right.

Mr. Bygraves wanted me to work with him, Jim Backus, and the staff in creating
some other character sketches that would be dropped in throughout the rest of the show.

GB told him that I only did the "three-way" routine but Mr. Bygraves insisted
that he wanted to use me in some other sketches. It was tense. I naively said to GB,
"What's the diff?" He knew he was being possessive and that it wouldn't serve him
well, so he acquiesced and I ended up performing in the other sketches.

We had days off in between when other people were rehearsing and that was when
we were going to go on our day trips to Brighton, Windsor Castle, Hampton Court, and

the like. But now that I was also working with Mr. Bygraves and Jim Backus, it was going to be necessary for me to also work on those days off. GB said no: We had plans for our days off. This meant that I had to rehearse my extra sketches while GB and I were in the studio for our bit. He would sit there and watch us rehearse and then all the way back into London tell me what I was doing that could be improved.

Things got worse. About two days after we got there, it started snowing so I went shopping on Carnaby Street and bought what I thought was a very cool sheepskin coat from Afghanistan with the fleece on the inside and the skin on the outside. It was really inexpensive, and I figured out why very soon afterward.

The coat had been cured in urine and smelled awful! I still wore it every day to the studio, but each night I would close the bathroom window on one sleeve and let it hang outside all night, thinking that maybe it would "air out." The aroma of the coat wouldn't change no matter what I tried. GB kept insisting that we were freezing our heinies off for nothing by leaving the window ajar.

Finally, one day as we were driving to the studio with Jim Backus (he was on the show with us), Jim turned to me and said, "You know what you should probably do with that coat? Just have it cleaned—and burned!"

There were snow flurries whirling and twirling under the streetlights at night when we came home from the studio, but there were also cars slipping and sliding in the unexpected snow. And then GB got the flu.

It seemed like he was sick forever with fever and chills, and there we were with all sorts of press events to attend and obligations to the show—not to mention the upcoming taping.

I finally had the concierge get a doctor, who prescribed some medicine that seemed to work. In the middle of all this, we got a telegram from Arlette and Daniel telling us that Ramona the cat had given birth to her kittens. This trip to London was becoming a series of unrelated, odd events—with the final one happening a few days before we left.

We'd finished taping the show and decided to do some fast sightseeing before we came home. We went and saw the changing of the guard at Buckingham Palace and then decided to end the day with a trip to Westminster Abbey. GB got out of one side of the car, I got out the other, the car pulled away—and we'd lost each other in the fog! We finally hooked back up at the hotel, agreeing that it was probably time to get back to America before anything else could happen.

■ ■ ■ ■ ■ ■ ■ ■ ■ ■ ■ ■ ■ ■ ■

Christmas

The 1969 Christmas celebration we arranged on our return to America was quite elaborate if one considers that we were these two who kept insisting that Christmas wasn't important to us. This Christmas, GB and I spent the holidays with my parents at their home in Northern California.

It was really an adventure for GB. Not just because my mother always really did it up with "theme" Christmas trees in every room and elaborate decorations. This was truly an adventure because it was the first time that I'd ever known GB to go anywhere he wasn't booked to entertain.

Just to get to my Mom's house required flying to San Francisco and then changing to a tiny airplane that would take you the rest of the way. Then once you were there, there really wasn't anything to do but eat Christmas cookies and take long walks in the woods and that was about it. GB knew this but came up there to meet me anyway.

Mother and I picked him up at the airport and brought him back to the house. Everything was moving right along. The soup was hot and there was plenty of ketchup. And there were also two dogs to play with. In addition to Prunsie (yuk!), there was a huge collie named Fanny (short for "Fantastic Dog"). We'd taught Fanny to get excited and bark when she heard the word "horse." This meant that every time Fanny walked through the room we would all yell, "Horse, Fanny!" Tolstoy writes in the opening lines of *Anna Karenina*, "All happy families are like one another; each unhappy family is unhappy in its own way." I'm still waiting to meet this other family that happily yells, "Horse, Fanny!"

GB, always a good mixer, joined in and pretty soon we had Fanny barking like crazy most of the time. (She loved it, honest.) This activity went on every day while we were there and, to coin a phrase, "a good time was had by all."

Now, here comes the goofy part. Even though he participated, GB didn't really understand what was going on. He told me on the plane coming home that if someone kept calling him a "Horse-Fanny" he would bark all the time, too. And why did we name such a beautiful dog "Horse-Fanny"? Need I say more?

There are pictures from that Christmas of GB holding one of the world's ugliest ties—which *I* had given him. I gave him ugly ties that Christmas—and he gave me a six-carat diamond ring that had belonged to Gracie. Not only was the ring wonderful-looking but it had a great story that went with it.

It seems that the center stone, which was more than four carats, was from a set of shirt studs and cuff buttons that belonged to "Poppa Burke," the husband of Gracie's Aunt Clara. Their marriage in itself was a story.

As a young girl, Aunt Clara lived in San Francisco before the turn of the century and fell head over heels in love with Poppa Burke, a fabulously wealthy man who was more than fifty years her senior and didn't know she was alive. To get his attention, she threw herself under the wheels of his carriage. Poppa Burke leaped out of the carriage (GB said Poppa Burke leaped as well as he could for "an old guy"), lifted her into his arms, and put her in the carriage. The next thing you knew, they got married and stayed married until Poppa Burke died when he was ninety-eight!

Pretty terrific story for a pretty terrific present! And not bad for a guy who doesn't believe in Santa Claus. I wore the ring during the holidays, but when we got back home I gave it back to him because I couldn't afford the insurance. Two years later he gave the ring back to me when I wanted to go to graduate school and told me to sell it to pay for my master's degree. I did! (P.S. He did wear the tie—but only once.)

After the trips to London and Northern California, we still hadn't finished our traveling for the year. We had a New Year's engagement in Miami to tape *The Jackie Gleason Show* during the week.

If London had seemed like an adventure and the trip up north an odyssey, this trip to Miami really sent the year out with a bang. We brought in the New Year while in the middle of a full-blown hurricane. It was so good to finally come home, get back into our old routine, and know we were going to be there for a while. Or so it seemed.

· SIX ·

"You really like school, don't you,
Kid? I don't get it but I want you to
do whatever makes you happy."

By the beginning of the summer of 1969, what I thought would make me happy certainly ended up not making GB happy. First of all, I wanted to return to Great Britain for a month with a girlfriend and backpack through England, Scotland, and Ireland. Second, I wanted to change colleges. The fact that I wanted to change schools wasn't such a problem except that the school I'd chosen required that I become a full-time student. At this point in my education I didn't really feel that I had a choice.

UCLA wasn't working for me in a lot of ways. I started out as an economics major but failed most of the required math classes. So I changed my major to English, but it never seemed as if I was able to take very many English classes because there were always so many other basic requirements.

The college that I'd found, Immaculate Heart, was nearby and it was possible for me to help design my own curriculum. But this ultimately meant that I would also create my own chaos.

After the trip that summer to England, which was great fun but certainly not eventful, I started at Immaculate Heart. Established in 1916, it had a reputation for being a sort of Catholic girls' seminary/finishing school. It certainly was a finishing school for me: It finished my relationship with GB as it then existed.

At UCLA I'd been anonymous. The classes were huge, my personal business was my own, and I was content to keep it that way. Immaculate Heart was something else completely. It had barely 400 students and had recently become coed so there were now 360 female students and 40 male students. The topper was, however, that the nuns had recently left their order and theoretically broken away from the Catholic Church. They no longer wore habits, and were now wearing blue eyeshadow and trousers! Oh my!

This campus was no longer, by any stretch of the imagination, comprised of nice Catholic schoolgirls in uniforms or even in cashmere sweaters and pleated skirts being instructed by beatific, pious, sweetly smiling nuns who resembled Audrey Hepburn in *The Nun's Story*. Immaculate Heart had become a campus of, shall we say, "free thinkers."

With a double major in English and theater and a minor in music, I now spent most of my time at school, either practicing or, believe it or not, rehearsing. This immediately got in the way of my life at home. I'd usually just make it back in time for dinner. Sometimes I'd have to dash back to school for rehearsal. And when I was home I was always practicing the piano, which would drive GB crazy. He'd say to me repeatedly, "Kid, you practice the piano all day long and then your big finish is to timidly get up in front of an audience and play some piece of music that no one can hum when they leave!"

It wasn't just the piano that got me into trouble. It was the Theater Department that really took its toll. It was a very "advanced" theater program conducted during the days of *Hair, The Living Theatre, Dionysus in '69*, and anything else that involved taking your clothes off in front of an audience. Only I didn't want to disrobe onstage. I wanted to be in the chorus singing and dancing. I only wanted to read and study plays. I did *not* want to participate in what I considered "primal hoochie-koochie." But I was outnumbered at school and eventually made to feel as shallow as they come, with certainly no soul and an inferior intellect.

As the other students found out what my life away from campus was like, I was labeled a true anachronism. For some inexplicable reason, certain faculty members and students decided it was their duty to "raise my consciousness" and help me accept that I was living a very "sick and nonproductive" lifestyle, and that I was very likely being exploited by GB, who was taking advantage of my youth and lack of guile.

I tried to maintain my integrity through all of this in a myriad of ways. GB, not realizing the turmoil I was going through, was always there for me even though he seemed puzzled by it all. I auditioned and was cast in a very serious production of Ionesco's *Exit the King*. Fortunately, the student director, Tonda Marton, became aware of my feelings during our rehearsals and worked very hard to make me feel accepted and included. In fact, she's remained a close friend of mine ever since. But the play was very abstract for me.

GB felt the same way when he and my whole family and friends came to the performance. Afterward at a party he had for me at home, the only feedback that I really recall was my uncle's comment that, because my costume was a sleeveless gown, the great musculature in my upper arms was quite an asset.

One of my classes was this pseudo-intellectual class called Performance Theory, which dealt with such pithy questions as "What is the theater?" "What is the value of the text?" "Are directors truly necessary?" and "What is the responsibility of the actor?" GB came to school and we conducted a mock interview in which I put these questions to him in a very serious and intense manner. He responded in his own unique way—as a vaudevillian. The reception was less than lukewarm. Unfortunately, I myself thought maybe he had been a little too glib in his responses.

The part of the curriculum that became the kiss of death was the mandate to go see all sorts of avant-garde theater all the time. That was it. Between my practicing the piano, rehearsing, and going out, GB and I hardly saw one another anymore. GB, and I certainly don't blame him, got sick of my newly found expertise on just about any subject. This gave us plenty to argue about, which was something we'd just never spent much time doing before then.

That December, I told him I thought I should move out and "experience independence." Even though I was being a real pain in the neck, he still didn't want me to go. I self-righteously told him it was best for both of us. It probably really was for him—what a relief to no longer have to put up with any more of my newly acquired foolishness! But moving out, for me, was almost a disaster.

The first thing I felt I needed to do was to go into therapy because GB had done me severe emotional damage—according to others. I asked GB if I could borrow some money to see a shrink. He asked me what I was going to talk about and I said, "My life." He told me he figured that was safe for him since he was no longer a part of it. Ouch!

I explained to him that he had been a big part of it and that was why I was going. With that he wanted to know what he did to me that was so horrible except to love me. I told him it was *my problem.* He loaned me the money and I ended up with this awful, earthy shrink whose only reply to me after I'd spilled my puny guts was, "And what do *you* think about that, Melissa?"

I realized that I *knew* what I thought: My confusion had very little to do with GB and a great deal to do with the influence of the theater department. What unhappy, misguided, narcissistic, and probably minimally talented people! Some of them had obviously been severely brainwashed during their education. So I distanced myself, and it was during this time that I took up the harpsichord and refocused my studies in the music department.

This was also when I met my first husband. With only forty men on campus, dating was never an issue. There was none going on! But I'd asked my piano teacher if she knew of someone who could give me jazz lessons so I could learn to improvise, and she told me she knew just the person. Albin Konopka—a male.

During the late spring of '71 I started studying with Albin whenever possible. By the end of the winter semester, we were practicing Bartok Two Piano Music for an upcoming recital. He was very sweet but I was still very emotionally fragile. We finally started dating six months later. He was offered a scholarship to the Juilliard School in New York and asked me to come live with him. When I called my mother to tell her that that's what I was going to do, her response was, "You're stupider than I thought you were." So I did what was inferred to be the "smart thing"—I married him.

GB had met Albin earlier in the year at one of our recitals, but our engagement still came as a huge surprise to him—as it did to me! Of late, GB and I still spent a great deal of time together, went out to dinner together, and laughed together, even though I no longer lived at the house. I really didn't stop to consider the impact of what I was doing.

The process of getting a rather large wedding organized on such short notice became a Gothic nightmare in its complications.

First of all, Albin's parents didn't like me and were of no help. Oh well. Next, Albin was eligible for the draft and was trying to get out of it so he could continue studying piano. But there was nothing wrong with him. He'd gotten a job for the summer as a pianist that required him to go on the road, and I was left alone for the summer. It seemed that anything that could go wrong did, and every incident ended up being another omen of more disasters to come.

As GB held my hand through all of this, he never said a word. It was only years later that I realized he was using the technique on me that he himself explained to me for use in unpleasant situations: "If you think someone is involved with someone 'jerky' or is making bad choices, just keep your mouth closed. Your comments and pressure about the person or situation will only drive them deeper into it." I guess he figured that if I was in any deeper, I'd be six feet under. He was almost right.

■ ■ ■ ■ ■ ■ ■ ■ ■ ■ ■ ■ ■ ■ ■

Two nights before our wedding, Albin crashed my car by rear-ending someone on the Hollywood Freeway. My uncle offered to help Albin rent a car for at least the honeymoon. Honeymoon? Suddenly I had 20/20 vision concerning the future, but it was too late. I let my mother know I wasn't happy. She let me know that I "should have thought of this a long time ago" and, by the by, she would have gladly given me the money she was spending for this wedding so that Albin and I could have just simply gone off and quietly gotten married. Gee, too bad she never said that up front.

GB giving me advice during the reception.

I finally snuck to a phone and called GB, sobbing. He listened patiently as usual and finally told me, "Kid, as long as you've got your pants down . . ." I knew what that meant.

There was a wedding. Albin and I did get married. There was champagne, dancing, and wedding cake. GB drank too much and then asked me to dance. He immediately asked,

"Why'd you do it, Kid?" and I unhappily whispered in his ear, "GB, we've gone over this a hundred times! You always told me to make something of myself and I figured that after graduating from college, the next thing would be to get married."

We both just looked at one another, and then Jack Langdon drove him home. My friend Tonda removed her girdle at some point and left it in the ladies' room—where she'd been holding court while recovering from a month of strict dieting that didn't accommodate the sudden imbibing of copious amounts of champagne. The management returned it to my mother the next day. I think that says it all. Oh, and Lee gave my mother a rather large emerald and diamond ring to match her green silk mother-of-the-bride dress.

I was married on September 24, 1972, but after the honeymoon I stayed in Los Angeles while my new husband went on to New York to begin graduate school. I wanted to oversee the repair of my car, and then I thought I would drive it to New York myself. In reality, I couldn't bear to leave GB. We'd never been separated by more than four miles, so the thought of being separated by three thousand was terrifying. I came back from my honeymoon and lived with GB for the next three weeks until I went back East. But only a part of me went to New York. My car stayed in GB's garage and Ramona the cat stayed in his bedroom.

·SEVEN·

"Make sure of what you think you want, Kid. Knowing you, you'll probably get it."

For the next three years Albin and I lived in New York and Paris. These times were often filled with conflicting emotions, and out of habit I always included GB in on every detail of it. Out of habit, he always participated.

GB and I began to send letters as soon as I got to New York. Actually, it started before I got there because I wrote him a thank-you note as soon as I got on the plane. For the next three years, we corresponded on a twice-a-week basis, which eventually became augmented with Sunday phone calls.

During this time, when I kept telling him how much I loved getting his letters, how much I loved him, and how much the letters meant to me, he used to say, "Kid, save all these letters. They could be money in the bank!" It wasn't until years later that I realized what he was saying. All I knew at the time was that they were a huge deposit in my spiritual and emotional bank account. The letters were always sweet, concerned, supportive, wise without being didactic, not to mention cheery and *very* funny, although the funny part sometimes seemed questionable. You see, sometimes I'd have friends read what I thought was an especially unique point of view or observation; when they were through they'd give an obligatory chuckle but I could tell they didn't quite get it. It still seemed that sometimes GB and I were the only people who got *our* jokes.

GB knew before I did that I would have a delayed reaction about this move to New York. I really had no idea what I was getting into. I thought I was getting what I wanted and doing what I had to do. I expected to be independent. GB's letters to me eventually became a kind of lifeline as I struggled to figure out what I was really doing. And then, when I started to see what I'd created for myself, my contact with him in the form of the letters and the phone calls and occasional visits became the life jacket that kept me afloat until three years later when I finally let him rescue me again.

The first apartment Albin and I had was in a brownstone on the Upper West Side. The first thing I noticed about it was that the heating system was not very reliable. None of our furniture had arrived from Los Angeles and so for a time we were sleeping in a sleeping bag. This was the beginning of a different kind of adventure for me. GB had warned me about how cold it could get back East, which was why he liked living in California. He took the first opportunity he could to remind me of this in his first letter.

October 27, 1972

I got your nice card. Jack enjoyed it, Packy enjoyed it,
and so did I. It reads like you're very happy, which is
great. But I'm surprised that I received it. You have
the wrong address and the wrong zip code. . . .

. . . But I suppose when you're just married you've got
other things on your mind . . . especially when it's
snowing and cold in New York, and you've got no heat
in your apartment.

One of the running themes throughout our correspondence was Ramona the cat.
It seemed that in a way we spoke "through" her as a way to say things to each other
that we couldn't say directly. In that same letter he wrote:

Anyway, everything is the same out here. Ramona
runs around the house screaming, "Mrs. Konopka!
Mrs. Konopka! Mrs. Konopka! Mrs. Konopka!"

The following was the usual ending of most of the letters, since GB always dic-
tated them to Jack while he was at the office.

Well, it's now 12 o'clock. If I don't get to the Club,
they'll be out of fish and my martini might be warm.

After Albin and I'd been in the apartment for about a month, the furniture arrived, including Albin's grand piano, which meant there was always music of some sort in the house. But I was bored. On the heels of boredom came homesickness. It sure didn't take long.

When I wrote to GB, I really had nothing to say and begged him to tell me what was going on at home. He wrote back one of his "goofy" letters that only *I* could appreciate and only *he* could write.

> October 30, 1972
>
> Got your nice letter, and evidently you sent it before you got the one I sent you after I received your postcard. Anyway, things are just about the same. The pool is clean, I'm still picking up the leaves, still go to the Club, but I switched from martinis to dry Rob Roys, which should make every newspaper in the country. That's a hell of a switch.

Now here is where GB went into one of his "goofy" story modes:

> Anyway, the house is running the same. Daniel and Arlette had dinner the other night in the Library and I waited on them. They complained that the soup wasn't hot enough. We all read your letter, and Ramona came

in. Ramona said, "Who's the letter from?" and I said, "Konopka." She said, "Where's that, near Glendale?" I said, "No, Lisa Konopka, she used to be Lisa Miller. You remember her," and Ramona said, "Oh, of course, we used to live together. How is she?" I said, "She's fine. She lives in New York now and she's sleeping with Albin." Ramona said, "She is! Well, I'm certainly not going to tell that to Princess [one of Ramona's kittens that I'd given to Arlette and Daniel], you know what a big mouth she's got." Then I went back into the kitchen, and Ramona and I had another Rob Roy, and she took my olive. Everybody is always taking my olive.

I'm doing "The Merv Griffin Show" tonight, but I don't know when it will be on the air. Georgie Jessel is on it and so is Connie Stevens, so it should be fun. I also did the Steve Allen show, "I've Got a Secret." I don't know when it's on the air either, but it turned out to be very funny. . . .

. . . You said you were going to look for a job. I think it's a great idea. It'll give you something to do instead of just running around New York buying shower curtains. . . .

> . . . Well, that's it. It's an abrupt finish, but you know
> me, I've never had a finish.

The only other "regular" job I'd ever had was during my last semester at Immaculate Heart. I'd gone to the school employment service and followed up on a listing to work for an architect as an assistant bookkeeper two days a week. The only thing I knew about making book was what I'd learned in Vegas!

I had kept that job for the entire semester. It had been great because the offices weren't far from Hillcrest, so I'd go have lunch with GB most afternoons. Then I got cast in the Los Angeles company of *Godspell* at the Mark Taper Forum. With this bit of luck, I quit the job and went directly into rehearsal when the semester was over in December. That was my job experience behind a desk. But this didn't stop me now. I knew how to type and I had a college degree so I figured, "How hard can it be?"

Harder than I had imagined.

> November 8, 1972
>
> I got your letter, and I'm sorry you haven't found a job
> yet, but maybe this might help. Enclosed find a letter
> that I've written to Louis Weiss. After you receive this
> letter I'd wait a day or two before you call him so it's
> not right on the nose. I'm sure he'll try to do
> something for you, I know he will. . . .

. . . Anyway, I hope this works and when you call
Louie use the name of Lisa Miller. Then when you get
to be a star you can change it to Konopka. That's
easier to remember than Miller. . . .

P. S. I'm glad your furniture arrived. Now you won't
have to sleep on the floor anymore. You can take your
sleeping bag and put it on the bed and sleep in it.

GB sent the following letter to Louis Weiss, his nephew, who was the head of the
William Morris Agency at the time. But by this time I had landed a job and was now
faced with some important decisions because this letter was certainly a letter of
introduction and an opportunity that only a foolish person would ignore.

November 8, 1972

Dear Louis,

This is a surprise--a letter from your old Uncle Nathan
Birnbaum. Remember me? I used to be in show business.

Anyway, here's the reason for this note. I don't know
whether you met Lisa Miller when you were out here,
but she got married and moved to New York a couple
of weeks ago. She worked with me in Vegas, and she

also did "The Jackie Gleason Show" with me, and Bob
Hope['s show] and "The Dean Martin Show." . . .

. . . If it's at all possible, Louie, please do something for
her. She's a hard worker and she loves show business.

And to show you what a kind uncle I am, you don't
have to split the commission with me.

Love to you and your family.

What I decided to do was stay with my job and try to do the other in my "spare"
time. Spare time came sooner than I thought. The man I worked for was a patroniz-
ing Park Avenue tycoon and my job was to call for his lunch, call for his limousine,
call his wife Bunny for him, and with all this calling I was also responsible for updat-
ing the Rolodex *and* hiring the temps since he went through secretaries as fast as he
went through his mail. One of the temps told me she had a much better job for me
through the New Year working in publicity for the Frazier–Foreman Heavyweight
Fight. I gave notice.

I was able to go to the William Morris office during my lunch hours because the
new job was just around the corner. And when needed, I could skip lunch and leave
an hour early in order to go to an audition.

GB's response to my new schedule was, as always, supportive. The letter was also
in the goofy category since Jack Langdon was on vacation, leaving GB and his writer
Elon Packard on their own.

November 15, 1972

Jack Langdon will be gone for two weeks . . . so I'm
really typing this letter myself. No I'm not. If I was
typing it my spelling would be very bed. (Dear Lisa: This
is Packy. I'm typing it and my spelling is very bed two.)

In your letter you told me you were working, which I
think is great. It'll give you something to do while Albin
is studying at Juliarde. (Packy again. I didn't know how
to spell Juliarde so George just spelled it for me.)

Then he proceeded with the usual cold-weather joke:

Also in your letter you said it was very cold in New
York. This should be great for you and your husband
'cause when you're cold you get to be great lovers.
I've lived in a warm climate, January will be thirty-
one years. . . .

. . . I hope Louis Weiss can do something for you. I
know he'll certainly try.

Since it was almost Christmas, and since GB and I always made attempts to down-
play the holidays, this year was no exception although we weren't even in the same state:

You know I'm not much for holidays so I don't know
what to do about you for Christmas. You know what I
do for everybody else--I give them a bottle of brandy.
But now that you live in New York, there might be
something there that you need . . . if Albin reads this
letter, tell him not to get upset because I've known you
for a long time. . . .

P. S. Make sure you hold on to your job 'cause I think
it's important to keep busy.

The unspoken part of that P. S. was "hold on to your job because it may be a while
before an acting job comes through!" But GB's next letter did enclose a copy of the
return letter to him from Louis Weiss to prove that GB was doing all he could for me
(see facing page).

Since I was always begging for news of what was going on at home, GB included
a description of Sandy, his daughter, and her family's move to Northern California
(not that far from where my mother lived). I couldn't imagine that he'd made another
pilgrimage to Northern California, but his description of it speaks volumes about what
he thought of it:

November 29, 1972

I just got back from Coloma where I visited Sandy and

GEORGE BURNS

November 22, 1972

Dear Lisa:

This is just a short note to let you know that I heard from Louis Weiss and I'm sure he'll do anything he can for you.

I'm enclosing the letter he sent me so you can take it from here.

Happy turkey,

Love -
G. B.

Steve at their trailer camp. It's impossible to explain.
They work like dogs around there. They run a big
market which is attached to the front of their house and
Sandy takes care of it because Steve is out building
cottages. She waits on customers in the store and pumps
gas at the station they have in front. It's a big project
and very rustic. It won't be completed for three years.
The fog rolls in in the morning and you freeze your
heinie off. To pump gas with a cold ass isn't the greatest.

GB's career was slowly starting to pick up and he was thrilled. Between that and
him trying to jump-start mine, much of our correspondence was devoted, as usual, to
show business.

Now for a little news that I got a kick out of. I just got a
letter from the Buddah Record people and I'll quote it
verbatim as it's very short and it gave me quite a thrill.
It says--

Dear George:

We figured out that you must have been ahead
of your time, so we're gonna try it one more
time. I've sent you some albums under

> separate cover. Perhaps we'll come through
> this time
>
> Best regards,
>
> Neil Bogart (President)

Oh, no! Not that record again. It didn't sell the first time, but at least this time I wouldn't be involved.

He closed this letter by also bringing up something else from the past:

> Now for some news that'll make your hair stand on
> end. (And for God's sake, don't let Albin read the rest
> of this paragraph.) I just had the bottom of my pool
> painted. AND I put a little brick wall around those
> three orange trees. . . .

He was referring to the remnants of our disastrous Fourth of July pyrotechnic display.

For me, things had settled into a routine. William Morris had me meet with an agent who had been in the business for years. She had a vocal coach for me who became a dear friend and very helpful to Albin. She decided that commercials would be just the thing for me while I was auditioning for other work. But she was also an insufferable snob. She closed her pitch to me about doing commercials with,

"But of course, *our* girls don't do deodorant commercials!"

Of course not. We wouldn't do that when we could be swigging and swooshing mouthwash or running our tongues over our teeth and saying "M-m-m-m" to indicate that our teeth were deliciously clean.

The best thing about this period was that Albin wrote some great arrangements for me to use at auditions. How lucky I was to have a built-in rehearsal and audition pianist!

In spite of all the vocal training I was always going through, GB continued to heckle me about his record whenever possible. In the next letter he continued:

> December 5, 1972
>
> I got your nice letter, and the first thing I did was give Packy a raise for his excellent typing. Of course, I'm taking it out of Jack's salary.
>
> Right now I'm waiting to get a call from Neil Bogart of Buddah Records. I want to know what they're doing with it. I'll keep you in touch, because you were the contractor for that vocal group, <u>nebbech</u>!

Nebbech is a Jewish word for putz. He called me a *putz*! He still loves me! Then he softened it with:

> P. S. If you get lonesome and want to speak to

Ramona, just reverse the charges. She said she'd pay
for it. She's a very generous kitty.

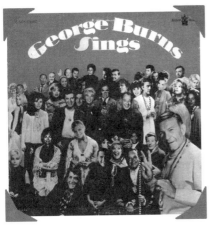

GB's first album in twenty years.

The Sunday phone calls started. He
would usually call me on Sunday afternoon and if he didn't I'd call him collect
when I knew he was having his martini.

The next letter contained great news.
GB was coming to New York at the end
of January to do a concert at Avery
Fisher Hall. Knowing that he was coming certainly made being separated during the holidays easier. GB seemed preoccupied with what should go on during
the holidays:

December 12, 1972

Enclosed find a little check. It should take care of the
pictures and the boots. If there's anything left over,
buy Albin some brandy and Sylvia the cat some kitty
litter. Make sure they don't get mixed up. If you do,
you'll have a cat that's drunk and a husband who's
pooping. . . .

> . . . Anyway, we all miss you. The house is getting to
> be Christmasy with the lights on the mirrors and the
> tree in the hall. New Year's Eve I might have a few
> people at the house. Sorry you and Albin won't be
> here.

He just wouldn't let go worrying about it, although we certainly never had before.

> December 13, 1972
>
> I'm dictating this to Jack over the phone, because I
> want to let you know not to send me any Christmas
> present. Don't knock yourself out, because I don't need
> anything. Just send me a card. Don't forget now, don't
> buy anything for me.
>
> I told Jack he could sign this.

Then Jack added something which began the "stamp secret" where he would always enclose a healthy supply of stamps in all my letters:

> Dear Lisa,
>
> Hi, Kid. I know it's near to Christmas so here are

more stamps. I don't have any Christmas stamps, so
Eisenhower will have to do. But as George says, that's
show business.

Not a word now--our secret.

The letter that came right before Christmas said nothing but we knew it said
everything. The second paragraph is really GB's way of saying that he was glad I'd
stopped whining for awhile and was staying very busy. And he was right. It really was
much better than complaining. The rest of the letter was designed just to make me
smile, and it did.

December 22, 1972

I got your letter on yellow paper and it was exciting, it
added a little color to your typing. You can't tell, you
might work yourself up to where you're using pink
paper.--Well, that's my opening line, I'll try to do better
as I continue writing. . . .

. . . Your job sounds great. You're paid for your lunch
hour and now you've got an answering service,
handled by the Morris office, and you're having
pictures taken--I'm surprised you have time enough to

promote the Frazier-Foreman fight. . . . I think I'm
going downhill, I liked my opening line about the pink
paper bit. . . .

. . . I got a call from Tonda, and she said she was going
to New York, and if I had anything for you, she'd be glad
to take it. So I told her I had about six pounds of kitty
litter, and she hung up. I guess she hates animals. . . .

. . . What's going on between you and Jack, that
you know, that Jack knows, and that I don't know?

. . . Yes, I've got a Christmas tree, the same like last
year with the four little angels standing in the front of
the mirror, and when you wind them up they say,
"three cheers for Jesus." It's a hell of a way for a Jew
to spend the holidays. . . .

. . . Ramona and I send our love. That gives you the
idea--I've been in show business all my life and a cat
gets top billing.

Christmas wasn't very interesting. Albin and I went to the movies and had cold
chicken when we came home. There were decorations and I did bake Christmas
cookies but it didn't really seem like Christmas without the usual activities. We were

in a holding pattern, waiting for GB to keep us filled in on the re-release of the old album and the upcoming concert. Spending time with him was still the priority. My job with the Frazier-Foreman fight was going to be over in the middle of January, so when GB got to New York I could spend all my time with him.

His next letter reconfirmed his excitement about the upcoming activities:

> December 29, 1972
>
> Your picture's on my desk, and when I leave at
> 12 o'clock Jack puts it on his desk. So I have it in
> the morning, and he has it in the afternoon. And last
> Tuesday, Packy asked if he could take it home. Jack
> and I said no. We thought he might scratch it.
>
> Well anyway, New Year's Eve at my house I've
> practically got your whole family. There's Phil and
> Andi, Graham and Laurel, and Mindy and her brother,
> and his girl. So we'll be thinking of you.

Here comes show business:

> We had a meeting with the Buddah people . . . Neil
> Bogart, the President of Buddah, and a couple of others.
> And it looks like everything is set, but there are some

loose ends that have to be tied together, so we're
waiting. But if I do the show, it's not going to be easy.
Although I'm doing some of the routines I've done
before (naturally you'd have to when you're doing
about two hours) but at my age my memory isn't what
it used to be. Neither is my . . . my . . . my . . . I'm still
smoking, though. . . .

. . . I'm also sending you a single which the Buddah
people have put out. I personally thing it's pretty good.
In fact, I think it's great. Oh, what's the use of kidding,
it's sensational! So what happened, when we worked in
Vegas we amounted to nothing. Now you're in New York,
you've got a husband, you're taking singing lessons,
you've got your own exchange, and here I am after all
these years I've got a chance to get into show business.

Always a dig about show business; always followed by something nice:

It was nice talking to you on the phone. Jack and I both
enjoyed listening to you. You sounded very good--up and
gay. And I think you'll love the Catskills. There are a lot
of Jews up there, nice people--I mean the Jews.

Albin and I had been invited to spend New Year's with some friends from college. The Catskills we went to must not have been the ones GB was talking about because it wasn't a great time! And now for one last bit—always looking out for me!

> Just thought of something. You said you're coming out
> in April to get your car. Well, if you're thinking of
> driving back alone, don't. I think it would be a very
> dangerous thing for you to do. If you can get somebody
> to go with you, then fine. . . .

This letter also included this note from Jack:

> December 29
>
> Here are some more stamps--and shhhh! It's still
> our secret.
>
> Regards,
> Jack

We were getting close to countdown and GB's enthusiasm was certainly contagious. By now Albin had gotten work from my vocal coach writing vocal arrangements and was now not only going to school but also practicing the piano eight hours a day. I was in limbo. And we were all waiting for GB.

January 12, 1973

We're all excited about the concert here. We're working our heinies off, and naturally we hope it's a smash. . . .

. . . Well, this is it because I've got to go over to Universal and look at some film. I'll be seeing you and Albin shortly.

I knew from talking to GB on the phone that he was really, really busy but it wasn't until he put it on paper that I realized what that meant. Also in this letter there were bits of information that I guess GB wanted to make sure I knew before he got there. One is not having "time" to see Pamela. Ever since I'd moved out he'd had a series of dinner companions and sometimes I even accompanied them on Thursday nights out. I always got a wicked sort of pleasure out of those dinners because the girl of the moment would be obviously miffed that I was there, and GB and I

Every morning GB would go for a swim.

would share laughs over all our private jokes. I never found any of these women to be a threat because I knew that what GB and I had between us was very different. As I remember, Pamela didn't last very long and from the sound of this letter it sounded like she was on her way out.

> January 19, 1973
>
> This is going to be a short note, because I haven't even got time to say hello to Pamela. . . .
>
> . . . Now--Louis Weiss is here, and I spoke to him, and I told him to get on that girl's heinie who is handling you and have her get you a job. He said he would as soon as he got back. . . .
>
> . . . Saturday is the 20th, I'm 77, I'm still swimming, still smoking, still singing, and I haven't got time to say hello to Pamela.
>
> . . . I'm going to do "The Merv Griffin Show" on the 8th, I don't know when it shows in New York, and then the Johnny Carson show on the 12th, which shows on the 13th in New York. Then Jack Benny and I are doing the Ann-Margret special on the 23rd. And then, of course, there's my concert. I'm so gaddmmned busy

I haven't got time to dictate this thing to Jack, let
alone say hello to Pamela. . . .

. . . Give my best to Albin, and I hope the janitor likes
my sweater. Ramona told me this morning, "When you
write to Lisa give her my love."

Two more weeks. I knew deep down what I really wanted while he was here: I
wanted to escape the life I had created for myself and go back to what I'd had. But I
now had what I'd thought I wanted and was too stubborn to admit I'd made a mistake. The final paragraph of this letter gave me such a sense of nostalgia. A dinner
party at 21 just like old times:

January 31, 1973

Cathy brought over your new pictures, and I think
they're just great. You know I always loved you
with straight hair. Remember in Chicago I tried to
straighten out your little curls.

Oops! Not another reference to that awful permanent in Chicago. He would never
let me forget it.

I'm glad you got an extra week's work, and I loved

your last paragraph in your letter where you said
you wowed them at the William Morris office and you
had to see the woman Friday. I hope she does
something for you. Sometimes it takes a long time.
Look at me, it took me 77 years. When you're 77
you'll have gray curls.

I arrive in New York on the 13th on TWA Flight 904,
arriving at 4:54 P.M. When you meet me try to have
Albin with you because I've got some heavy luggage.
But my music I'm going to carry. . . .

One of GB's running jokes for as long as I knew him was, "Kid, when I go, I'm taking
my orchestrations with me!"

P. S. Saturday night, the 17th, Carol Channing and
Charlie Lowe are giving a party for Jack Benny and
myself. Naturally, you and Albin will be invited. I'm
sure it will be informal.

All that was next was SHOW TIME!

·EIGHT·

"Don't forget, I didn't amount to anything until I was 77. But if you can't make it by the time you're 77, I think you should look for something else."

Having GB in New York was the best. It was like old times: the rehearsals, press conferences, phones ringing, and GB in the best of spirits. Albin and I went to the hotel each morning for breakfast and I would stay and spend the rest of the day with GB. I'd go home in the late afternoon, shower and change clothes, wait for Albin, and then we'd both go back together for dinner or whatever else was happening.

GB had a piano put in his suite so there was always something going on. Larry Fallon was there most of the time and when he wasn't, Albin was playing the piano. GB arranged for me to have a batch of tickets to give to my various acquaintances, including a couple of Albin's teachers from Juilliard (it was good PR for Albin).

When we had gotten to New York that fall, Albin had auditioned and been chosen to study with Rosina Lhevinne, a very revered and also very old piano teacher. Her husband was the late Josef Lhevinne, a very famous concert pianist and teacher. She was now the matriarch of the piano department. Because she was in her nineties at the time, students took lessons with one of her two assistants. The one Albin had the first year was an unmitigated snob whose wife (who also taught at Juilliard) had delusions of grandeur. I invited them to the performance. My mistake. Their front row seats did not impress them, nor did the show. Their mistake. The rest of us had a great time and the show was a raving success.

It was a difficult time when GB flew back to California. His first letter to me after he returned really came as a surprise, as did the letter from Jack Langdon that preceded it.

MEMO FROM JACK LANGDON

2/27/73

Guess the concert was a huge success. Everybody
I've talked to at Buddah seems to be very happy
and satisfied. George has been singing your praises
about how helpful you were to him in New York, and

how you kept him from those evil extra drinks before
a performance. Good for you, Kid. . . .

. . . Now, young lady, our secret (the stamps) is no
secret anymore. You must have blabbed. Oh well, I
guess it doesn't really matter--just because George got
mad at me and knocked one of my front teeth out (ask
him if I'm not missing one). But just to show you what
a swell guy I am, and what a real old poop George is, I
have stolen some of his stamps and am enclosing them
for your benefit.

GB always drank when we performed but he usually drank Scotch because gin
was "too tough." At twenty years old all of it was "too tough" for me! And I did know
that when we played Vegas and did two shows a night for a month at a time, sometimes his timing seemed off musically. I always figured I just didn't understand what
was going on, but there was a lot of drinking now that I think about it. And so what?
It certainly never interfered in our relationship and GB lived to be over 100 and
worked until he was 99!

I loved Jack's take about the stamps and GB finding out. He was starting to make
up stories as outrageous as GB's!

Several days after Jack's letter arrived, there was a letter from GB in the mail. It
was so heartfelt and sincere. Of course, it contained all sorts of news about what he

was doing, but there were some definitely personal touches about his life and our continuing friendship:

> March 1, 1973
>
> I got your nice letter, and it was just as nice for me to see you as it was for you to see me (and I got to know Albin better, and you're married to a nice fellow). But I've got to give you credit, if it wasn't for you, the concert might not have been a hit. It was you who made me lay off the booze, which I can't thank you enough for.

He continued on a much lighter note—filling me in about work—but couldn't resist getting back to *us*:

> I'm going to Vegas this coming Monday with Jack Benny to do the Ann-Margret special, and then I'm coming back on Wednesday for a stag dinner given by the Friars for Army Archerd, Jim Bacon, Hank Grant, and Vernon Scott. We just finished writing a dirty speech that I've got to memorize. It's not exactly dirty, it's filthy. When you give a dinner for one man, you

can get dirty, but when it's for four, you have to dip
your pen in your heinie to write it. You're too young
for me to say ass. . . .

. . . I was waiting for all these years to have you admit
that I finally knew what was good for you in Vegas,
but you wouldn't listen. So now that I've said I told
you so, Ramona just bit me. . . .

. . . I think I've had it with Pamela. The only one I've
got left is the bombshell, Lita Baron. But Lita's a nice
girl and she's good company. . . .

. . . Anyway, it was fun seeing you and Albin, and you
never know what's around the corner. I might not see
you for months, and then again I might see you next
week. . . .

. . . But Lisa, I do want to thank you for everything
you did for me in New York. I appreciate it very much.
You're a darling girl.

That last paragraph says it all. It wasn't just everything I did for him in New York. It was everything he'd done for me for years no matter what my choices were. I may have been a "darling girl" but he was a truly special man.

Right after GB left I came very close to getting a really good acting job and had gone through numerous callbacks only to eventually not get it. I was so disappointed because I was really beginning to appreciate New York and would have enjoyed working. Also at that same time Albin had decided that we should return to Los Angeles for the summer so he could take a piano master class at USC with Madame Lhevinne. When I told GB both bits of news, he had the right things to say in both instances:

> March 5, 1973
>
> It was nice talking to you the other day, and sorry that you didn't get that job. In fact, we're all sorry you didn't get that job. But keep punching, Kid, something must happen. Don't forget, I didn't amount to anything until I was 77.
>
> . . . It will be nice to see you again. I told Jack that you were coming out here this summer--no, I didn't tell him, he just found out. I'm sure you'll be able to find something out here. If not, I'll give you a job taking care of Ramona Miller. All you got to do is brush the kitty. I could have said brush the pussy, but I'm too dignified for that sort of stuff.

Of course, next he moved on to his career, which I was soon to be a part of for the summer.

> I was supposed to go to Las Vegas today to do the Ann-
> Margret show, but Jack Benny has got a cold, he's in
> bed, so it looks like I might have to cancel, which is too
> bad because it was a very easy show to do. But they're
> trying to get Bob Hope to take Jack's place, so I'm
> sitting in the office twiddling my thumbs waiting for
> the phone to ring. But I'm having fun. I'm at the age
> now where twiddling is enjoyable, but I must admit
> that one thumb doesn't twiddle like it used to. If you
> heard this routine, tear up the letter.

Even though I was looking forward to going home for the summer, I was getting very discouraged auditioning. I kept getting so close and then not getting it. I think I knew that my heart wasn't really in it, but at some level some part of me still was. I suppose it was the part of me that didn't want to disappoint GB.

He devoted almost all of his next letter to trying to buck me up, which I really appreciated because I knew how busy he was.

> March 12, 1973
>
> I enjoyed talking to you Sunday, but I was sorry you

were so depressed, and your letter was on the gloomy side, too. Oh well, there's one thing that's encouraging about it, it can't get any worse, so it's got to get better. And if I know you, you'll keep trying. . . .

. . . But you know, we were talking about you in the office this morning, and we all came to the same conclusion--you should try to be an actress first, and your singing and dancing would be a by-product of that. We all think you read lines very well. So if I were you, that's the thing I'd look for. And if you look for a job as an actress, you'll probably wind up getting a job as a singer or dancer. That's the way the ball does something . . . it bounces, that's it . . . that's what the ball does. . . .

. . . Again don't forget I'm 77 and I, too, am looking for a job as a dramatic actor. I've made people laugh, they've heard me sing, and now I want to make everybody cry. After I've done that I might stick a feather in my heinie and marry Gladys Trueblood.

With this letter, I felt like I could keep going. I asked my singing teacher about someone to study with while I was in Los Angeles. He said he knew just the person and made a few calls to get me into this exclusive musical comedy workshop. Now I had that to look forward to for the summer. I started working very hard to get my voice in shape and I doubled up on my dance classes. Keeping so busy was just what I needed and I forgot that maybe I didn't want to be doing any of this!

I was busy. Albin was busy. And GB was very busy. It seemed as if there wasn't much going on of special interest in L.A. Maybe that's why I got a series of "goofy letters" that didn't mean anything but did keep the two of us in contact.

March 20, 1973

I've got about five or six minutes before I go out to Forest Lawn, so this is not going to be a very gay note. It'll be just six minutes of nothing. . . .

. . . It was nice to talk to you, and I hope it stopped snowing. And I certainly hope the storm doesn't move west because it could wipe out my alfalfa crop. I never told you about my alfalfa crop, did I? If you're interested, ask me about it sometime.

How is Albin?

A photographer came into the room, his name is Sandy Field, and he's taking some pictures while I'm writing this letter, so I'm posing and smiling, but my heart isn't in it because I'm worried about my alfalfa crop.

Well, how is Albin? You didn't answer me before.

Well, I've got to go now, I've got to call up the florist and make my monthly visit.

But I've got a great closing line:

How's Albin?

P. S. You'll notice that your husband is doing better than you are. I only mentioned your name once. I mentioned him three times.

GB hadn't made up any Ramona the cat stories in a long time, which I'd mentioned to him when we'd last spoken on the phone. He took care of that in the next letter. He also told me a startling bit of news about his son.

April 6, 1973

Ramona loves me so much that I have to hide. No matter where I go she's on my lap. But at night I close my bedroom door, I don't let her sleep with me. I'm too old for catting around. . . .

. . . Ronnie and Peggy I think are getting divorced.

I guess that meant that Ronnie and his wife wouldn't be having Thursday dinner with us!

> They're at the point now where they both have lawyers. But whether Ronnie is upset or not, that you never know. I took him for dinner last night, and he's full of smiles, he's still on his toes, everything is wonderful. If his house was burning down, he'd say, "Good, let's toast marshmallows." He's as happy as if he'd found another country to buy. At least that's the way he acts. . . .
>
> . . . If you run into Albin, don't hurt him, give him my best.

The letter closed with a P. S. from Jack:

> P. S. Hi, Kid. The stamps are my idea. They are a bribe to keep you quiet in case the piano is out of tune when you get here in June. You know it will be.

A couple of days later I received a very sweet note about a bracelet that GB had given me.

April 9, 1973

This is just a little note. I happened to read in the
paper today that a $20 gold piece is now worth $147.
I gave you a bracelet with a lot of little gold coins on
it, so I think that's now worth quite a bit of money.
Just don't let it lay around the house, because it's as
good as cash. This is just to remind you to be careful
and don't be careless with it.

Over the years GB had given me some exquisite jewelry and the bracelet he talked
about was really one of my favorites. It was a very heavy gold link bracelet with a selection of very old American gold coins on it. There were also several other beautiful gold
bracelets and necklaces that always made me feel very special when I was wearing them.

Albin and I were now in the midst of subletting our apartment and scouting for
a place to live in L.A. His parents had an extra car they were going to loan him for
the summer, and, of course, I had the famous car stored in GB's garage.

April 13, 1973

Understand you put in a long-distance call for me
yesterday, and I wasn't in the office. I hope you haven't
got a problem, but if you have, we'll talk about it
Sunday. Of course, this will arrive probably on Monday

or Tuesday, and by then if you've got a problem, I'll
know what it is. And if you haven't got one, ignore the
letter and the phone call. (Jack thinks this is a very
funny opening paragraph, so I told him to use it again
at the finish of the letter.)

. . . I don't think Arlette will let you go into the
kitchen after what you said about going to mess it up
when you get here. The kitchen looks like it should be
in Tiffany's window. . . .

P. S. I'm not going to repeat the first paragraph. Jack
read it again and he doesn't like it. And you know,
Jack makes all the decisions in this office. That's why
we're doing so well.

Albin had a bit of luck for the summer by offering to make himself available for
Madame Lhevinne as a baby-sitter when her nurse needed time off. Most of the other
students were not living very close to her so he was perfect. The trade-off was that
while he was there he'd get extra lessons. It was a really good thing for him. When I
mentioned it to GB, he responded with the following note:

May 3, 1973

I always enjoy talking to you on the telephone, and it

was nice to hear that Albin is doing arrangements and
baby-sitting with his music teacher. The nice thing
about that is you don't have to worry. If she's as old
as you say she is, he's really baby-sitting--unless she's
like my sister Goldie, who I think would enjoy Albin. In
fact, I think Goldie would enjoy me. Well, that's not
true--yes it is. . . .

. . . Well, that's about it, Kid. We're all anxiously
waiting to see you and Albin in June.

And I was anxiously waiting to see him, too. GB had already planned on what we
should do our first night in town, and it was not an option from the sound of this last
note before summer.

May 24, 1973

This is going to be very short because it's 6 minutes to
12, and when I get to the club there won't be any fish. . . .

. . . I'll see you Thursday. There's a new restaurant,
Gatsby's, out here, and that's where we're going for
dinner. It's very nice.

And it was, too, as was the whole summer.

·NINE·

"Don't let anybody upset you unless
you love them, and I know you
don't love your boss."

It was a great summer, although some things didn't turn out as I'd expected. I was supposed to work for GB in the office every morning. I'd drive over to his house and then drive with him to the office. But there were problems. His writers didn't seem comfortable with me around, and some days I wasn't able to have lunch with GB because I had my musical theater workshop in the afternoons. That also didn't turn out to be what I'd expected.

It turned out to be a sort of Broadway-meets-Los Angeles "You Can't Join Club." Just about everyone in it had worked on Broadway at one time or another and was an "actor who could sing." Because of this, the actual quality of the voices was negligible.

We were assigned obscure Sondheim and Porter songs that always included a "meaningful" verse. The man who created and ran all of this was very affected and used the words *amanuensis, eminent,* and *patently* at least once during every class. He also loved to make snide comments about vaudeville while glaring straight at me. In spite of all this, he was truly seductive in his beliefs that the skills he taught were unique and essential to be special on stage, and since all the students thought they personally were unique and special, they'd all come to the right place! Suckers! Me included.

I'd go over to GB's, put on my tape, and sing whatever song I'd been assigned, complete with movements and gestures. We'd both start laughing; I think that says it all. But to say on one's résumé that one had studied with this man was a definite plus.

The summer came to an end much too soon. We all went to Albin's recital with Madame Lhevinne's other students. Shortly after, Albin and I packed up our things and headed back East. The summer had truly revitalized me; for what I wasn't sure, but I knew I was ready to face New York again and my "other life."

During this next year, my car and GB's rapidly expanding work schedule became focal points of our letters.

October 29, 1973

The First National Bank requested a character
reference because you're opening a bank account. I

said you were reliable and honest and that you had
worked for me for the past four or five years--in case
they ask you, you'll know.

I'm also taking care of the insurance on your car--
and we also filled out information about you on your
unemployment--so after handling all your problems,
I've got no time left for show business.

That's not true. I just did "The Dean Martin Show,"
then I'm doing the Jack Benny special, and then the
George Schlatter special, which is called "One More
Time," and which is about all I've got left. "The Dean
Martin Show" will be on the air this Friday, November
2nd, but I think to see me you'll have to look fast.

And now for a little humor at someone else's expense:

I'm glad to hear that Larry Fallon left his wife. I know
he's on the make for everybody, so try to fix it up for
my sister Goldie. And if you run into Larry's wife, try
to fix that up for me. And tell her to fly out here fast.
As I said, I've only got "one more time."

Our letters became less frequent. GB was so busy working that we usually said everything to each other on the phone each Sunday. At the office during the week, everyone there was busy rewriting guest spots, upcoming commercials, and "the act," so letters to me weren't a priority.

No matter what was going on, I always wanted news of "home." It didn't have to be earth-shattering but just schmoozy and nice. . . .

> November 16, 1973
>
> I want to start by saying as soon as you're short of stamps let Jack know. I'm sure he will send them and won't let me know.

During that summer in L.A. I'd had GB's bedroom redecorated, since nothing had been done to it since the '50s and it had gotten really tatty. He kept telling me that it was too "swell" for him, but he certainly seemed to enjoy it for the rest of his life.

> My room is beautiful, but the bed is awfully high. This morning when I got up and stepped off I fell down. At night Daniel has to boost me into bed. Then when I get in I yodel for a few minutes. Well, that's enough of these facocktah jokes. It's really a lovely room, but I've got to keep the cats out of there. I don't want them breaking in my new carpet.

Then it was back to show business. GB was still actively doing what he could to help me:

> I'll be with Charlie Lowe Sunday, and Carol [Channing]
> is on the "One More Time" show, too, so I'll be on
> Charlie's heinie so that when they open in Philadelphia
> or Boston or New York, something will happen for you.

For me, it was back to singing lessons, dancing lessons, and general confusion. I just knew in my heart of hearts that at some point I'd have to admit that I didn't have the ambition to follow through on this "career." But I wasn't yet ready to do that, so I just kept going. I auditioned to sing in the choir for the Christmas concert at the Trinity Church on Wall Street. I got it, so that kept me busy with rehearsals for some time. Also, Albin and I had gotten our cat Sylvia (who had traveled to Los Angeles and back with us) a matching Persian boyfriend.

> November 28, 1973
>
> When I spoke to you on the phone you said you might
> come out here Christmas week. But if you're going to
> be one of the cherubs for the Trinity Church on Wall
> Street, I don't think you'll be able to come out. Being a
> cherub is a full-time job. . . .

> . . . I read your letter and you sound like you're
> busted, so I'll send you a little money. Now that you've
> got two cats, you've got to feed them. I'm not worried
> about you and Albin, but be sure you feed the cats.

I was really dragging along. I was still auditioning and not getting anything noteworthy. Albin, however, had gotten a job with an experimental production at the Brooklyn Academy of Music called *Candide* and he was now doing much better.

> December 6, 1973
>
> Just thought I'd drop you a little note to tell you
> that I sent Charlie Lowe a wire yesterday, he's in
> Philadelphia. Here's what I said: "George Schlatter
> called me and said the bit with Carol and me was
> sensational. Now what about Lisa Miller? I wish you
> would have somebody look at her because I think she
> would be a great asset in the chorus. Charlie, please
> do this for me. My love to that big talent you're
> sleeping with."
>
> Lisa, I can't do more than I did. I think he owes it to
> me and I hope he follows through. I must have talked
> to him six or seven times when he was here. Let's

hope this last wire works. If I hear from him, you'll
hear from me right away. . . .

. . . This letter isn't going to be too funny. In fact, it's
not going to be funny at all. I saw the Alan King
show last night, and it was nothing. As dull as
this letter is, compared to that show it should get
screams. And I ought to know, I was on it. I'm
glad you haven't got a television set, and after
seeing that show last night, I'm going to get rid of
mine, too. . . .

. . . The bed that I used to have, we put in the
other room. So if you come out here, you'll have
a nice bed to sleep in. It took a lot of years but
you'll finally be sleeping in my bed. I can't help it,
but this letter is getting funnier than "The Alan
King Show." . . .

It was an awful Christmas. Even though we both still professed to not like
Christmas, there was always a certain sweetness about it when we were together,
so it was, as usual, lonely for me without GB's participation. Also, my stepfather
Lee had been diagnosed with cancer; since he'd had it before, things didn't look
good.

December 17, 1973

. . . This is going to be short--really short--in fact, I've gone on too long already. I wasn't going to use that last line, I had a joke about me being short, but it's been kicked. In fact, for 77 years it's been kicked--but not lately.

Anyway, I spoke to you yesterday, and you know all the news. . . . Lee is feeling a lot better, your mother said she was taking care of herself. . . .

P. S. And if Jack wants to make this longer, he can. And if he can do it to the letter, I'll let him work on me, too.--Okay, so I'm a dirty boy!

P. P. S. from Jack--
And he is, too! But he has his nice moments!

To make myself even more miserable, I asked a lot of whiny questions about the holidays in my next letter to GB. He responded with a letter that obviously took time, thought, and love:

January 4, 1974

When Jack and I spoke to you on the phone Thursday you sounded sad. Well, do what I do. When I get up in the morning the first thing I do is sing "When you're smiling, keep on smiling and the whole world smiles with you." Try it, and if you don't feel good, try it anyway--only sing it off key. And, Kid, it could be worse. You're married, you got a nice husband who's going to run Rubenstein out of business one of these days, and then again you've got me, a very old mentor.

Anyway, I got your nice letter, and in it you say you want some questions answered, which I will, but I also got your card about coming out for my birthday. You better forget it, Kid, because I'm going to be 78 years old and I'm trying to forget it, too. In fact, I'm going to give a little party on the 20th and I'm inviting Lita Baron, Ronnie Burns, and George Pallay--and I'm not showing up. So you're not missing much.

Now for your questions: Question number one, how was my Christmas? It was great. Daniel and Arlette opened all my packages, I have yet to see them. I said Happy Birthday to Jesus and went to sleep.

Second question, did I miss you? Yes. I not only miss you on Christmas, I miss you all the time. Make sure that Albin reads that last line.

Third question, have I got a copy of <u>Playboy</u> yet? No, I haven't, and I don't know what it means. Am I the centerfold? If that last line isn't funny, Packy thought of it.

Fourth question, did I have roast turkey? No, I stayed with eggs and onions and a little barley soup.

Fifth question, did I kiss anybody under the mistletoe? No, I didn't kiss anybody under the mistletoe. In fact, I don't know what a girl's mistletoe is. I haven't seen one except my sister Goldie's, and that one needs retreading.

Sixth question, did I have some egg nog? I certainly did, with onions in them. I'm a Jew.

Seventh question, did Ramona give me a present? I got a beautiful tie from Carol Channing, and Ramona Boo-Booed on it, and the tie looks better. Well, that takes care of all your questions.

GB subtly let me know that he thought Albin was losing patience with our ongoing friendship:

I'm sure Jack has a few words to say, and a few stamps to go with them. And give my love to Albin,

and by the way, when I called you Albin answered the
phone and he said, "Do you want to talk to Lisa?" and
he didn't speak to me. Maybe the receiver was too
heavy . . . and I'm having trouble finishing this letter,
but us old mentors ramble on.

GB's letter was the wake-up call that I needed. I decided to keep on studying,
but I also decided to go back out and get a "real job." So I did. I was hired as assistant to the president of a children's book publishing company. I liked the books and
I liked the staff. The work was interesting in an odd sort of way.

About two months into the job, my boss asked me if I could type one of his man-
uscripts, which had nothing to do with our publishing program or my regular work.
Of course, I said yes. It turned out he was writing pornography on the side! Him with
his Yale pennant and canoe paddle from camp up on the wall. The next thing I
observed was that he had binoculars in his office and was often scanning the apartment house across the street from our offices when I walked in. I quit. It wasn't that
I was a prig. I was put off by the fact that he was so obtuse about it.

Because of this I really didn't have anything to tell GB when we talked, so he
made up stuff to write to me to fill up space:

February 19, 1974

Got your funny letter. . . .

. . . I told you about the Sinatra dinner on the phone.
I didn't tell you enough, it really was very, very
exciting. Sinatra went all out. Jack Benny never had a
party like that. Neither did anybody else. Edie Goetz
was there, and she said, "How's Lisa?" I said, "She's
fine. She's married to Albin Konopka and they're doing
great." That last line isn't true, I'm trying to pad out
the letter. . . .

. . . The Agnews were at the party with their daughter
Judy, who recently had her tonsils taken out, but she's
feeling fine now. Isn't that nice?

. . . I told you about Judy Agnew, didn't I?

I think I did. If I didn't, send the letter back and I'll
write another paragraph. Oh yes, Governor Reagan and
his wife Nancy were there. I was amazed, the Governor
is 6'2". I thought he was 6'1". And here's something
very few people know--he used to be a movie actor. . . .

. . . Anyways, I thought these things would interest
you. They did me. In fact, these tidbits excited me so
much Lita Baron got jealous because I didn't look at
her tidbits. She's got three. . . .

. . . Well, that does it. My love to you and Albin, but don't split it down the middle. Take 75% for you and 25% for Albin. . . .

P. S. Here's a little bonus tidbit, and after you read it tear up the letter because I don't want anybody else to see it: The Baltic Sea is the deepest inland body of water in the Western Hemisphere!!

P. P. S. Hi Kid! Here are your stamps. I was supposed to have mailed them to you on Friday, but because George was in Palm Springs I took the day off. Don't tell him, he doesn't know! He also thinks I already sent you stamps--it's our secret. If you blab about it, I'll tell everybody you had an affair with Janis Joplin.

By this time, Albin's show had gone to Broadway and he'd gone with it. And in June he'd receive his master's degree from Juilliard.

April 24, 1974

. . . This is going to be very short, and when I say short, I mean short. The word "short" is wide open for a joke, but I'm not going to use it because I'm going to keep this letter clean.

I'm glad to see that <u>Candide</u> won all those awards on
the Tony show.

Anyway, as I said, this is going to be a little note, and
it is. My love to you and Albin, and I've got to get back
to my concert. . . .

That spring, I decided that I had to get back to school. I knew that someday I was
going to need more formal education to be happy with myself. So I asked Jack to help
me gather all my college transcripts so I could apply to NYU's School of Education.
Jack, being the always sweet and helpful person that he is, gave me a hand.

May 16, 1974

I've got a lot to learn again. I have to go over the whole
script of the concert. And I made a record of those two
songs--"Simon Smith and His Amazing Dancing Bear"
and "Dayton, Ohio--1903." I think I told you about it on
the phone. But anyway, I was very happy with the tape.
In fact, everybody seems to think it's good.

Well, take care of yourself, Kid, and don't let your
[former] boss upset you. Don't let anybody upset you
unless you love them. I know you don't love your boss,
so just say "yes, sir" and do it. . . .

P. S. from Jack

. . . I got a notice that your transcript of records had
been sent out.

■ ■ ■ ■ ■ ■ ■ ■ ■ ■ ■ ■ ■ ■ ■ ■

There were no letters for almost all of the next year. We did spend a great deal of
time on the phone but were both so very busy that there didn't seem to be enough time
to write.

I'd actually been accepted to NYU. Classes were to begin in two days and I had
to register immediately, so I rushed downtown on the subway. I couldn't believe that
I'd been accepted after my intellect (and self-esteem) had been so brutalized at various times at Immaculate Heart.

I got down there and happily stood in front of the registrar who told me that the
cost of my fifteen units for the first semester would be a staggering $1575! How could
that be? UCLA hadn't been that expensive! I found out that UCLA is a state school
and NYU is a private university—hence the difference. I said I'd get back to them
the next day and I sadly went home.

What was I to do? Albin and I didn't have that kind of money. I resigned myself
to calling my mother because I knew she certainly had it—especially after my stepfather had passed away that spring and she inherited his estate.

After listening to her excuses for fifteen minutes while we were on my "dime," she finally told me that it just wasn't possible. I called GB and told him my situation. He responded, "How do you want me to send it to you, Kid?" That was it. And the next day the money was at Western Union—as was the money from my mother, which I immediately returned to her.

That fall, I started graduate school. And also that fall, GB had open-heart surgery.

How could it be? He'd been so healthy. I immediately flew home to see him. By the time I arrived, he was already feeling much better. In fact, he told me he was feeling better than he did before he had surgery!

What an odd twist of fate it was that GB's heart was good as new and Jack Benny's gave out.

·TEN·

*"Just take care of yourself. And
don't give up. Keep fighting, Kid.
Something is bound to happen."*

It had been four months since GB's open-heart surgery. Not only was he fine, but he
was getting ready to make his first film in fifty years, *The Sunshine Boys,* which was
to be the beginning of his second career. Albin was still doing *Candide* and apply-
ing for different grants to study music in Europe, and I was rehearsing for a show. I
didn't know about anyone else, but I still felt like I didn't know what I was doing
although I was well into graduate school.

Even though we still spoke on the phone every Sunday, it had been months since
I'd actually seen GB. He was coming to New York, and I was delighted about my forth-
coming "GB fix"! The correspondence was now usually between Jack and me because
GB was so busy.

March 19, 1975

Hi, doll, it's been a long time, but I still hear about
your activities from George. So you may be out of
sight. But you're not out of mind.

I wanted to let you know that George will be arriving
in New York on April 4th.

Hope your show is a grand ball and that Albin's
continues to pack 'em in. Out here all is go-go-go for
the little picture star.

GB came into town for filming and it was just like old times. He was still trying
to get me into show business even though I'd almost finished my master's degree.
While he was in town, he said he certainly wanted to make time to come see the show
in which I was appearing. During this time he was being dogged by a reporter named
Dotsen Raders, who was writing an article for *Esquire* magazine and asked if he could
attend my show with GB. He seemed like a nice enough guy at the time. But Raders
ended up presenting a most unflattering and untrue picture of our relationship. After
all those years of being so wary of the press, this was actually my first taste of dishonest journalism—but it was not to be my last, as I would find out many years later.

After seeing the show, GB decided that it would be a good idea for me to go back
to the William Morris Agency since they had offices in Europe.

May 12, 1975

Hi, Kid, how the hell are you? Buying your own
stamps these days? That's the only time I ever heard
from you. Boy, does that let me know where I stand.

Anyways, our Little Star wanted me to send you a
copy of the letter to Louis Weiss. You should wait
three or four days before calling him. The letter will
probably go out tomorrow (13th) because George isn't
here to sign it.

Best of luck, doll. (from Jack)

This was the last of GB's letters trying to persuade someone to give me a break.

May 12, 1975

Dear Louis--

Louie, you can do me a favor. Now I saw Lisa Miller in
that show downtown, The Letter, and I'd like to say
that she really has become a very good actress. She
doesn't expect you to hand her any jobs, all she wants
is the opportunity to audition for them. And being

you're my <u>favorite</u> nephew, and assuming you'd like to
keep it that way, see what you can do, Kid.

<u>The Sunshine Boys</u> opens at the Music Hall around
Christmas, and your <u>favorite</u> uncle might turn out to
be a big movie star. So if you can do something to help
Lisa, I might arrange for you to meet Linda Lovelace.

I'll have Lisa call you, Louie, and thanks for anything
you can do. . . .

That was it. From then on, Albin and I spent our time packing and trying to make
arrangements to move our household to Paris, sublet the apartment in New York, and
find storage for many of our things.

GB was still very busy back in Los Angeles with *The Sunshine Boys* and with
other incoming movie offers. The last letter I got in the United States was from Jack:

June 1975

Dear Kids--

I really do hope that all goes well for you over there. It
sounds very exciting. But when I think of you having all
those adventures and me sitting here at this typewriter,
the only word that describes my feelings is--MERDE!

(That's a very good French word for you to learn, Lisa. You can use it effectively on many, many occasions.) . . .

Trust me: For the ensuing months I did use that word, and some other words that had come into my vocabulary.

■ ■ ■ ■ ■ ■ ■ ■ ■ ■ ■ ■ ■ ■ ■

Somehow we got ourselves and many of our belongings—including Sylvia the cat (now by herself again) and two thousand pounds of possessions—to Paris. After bumbling around for a few weeks, we all got settled—me, Albin, and my cousin Mindy, who'd just graduated from college and was going to live with us for the year.

One of the first things I bought was a transformer so that I could start typing letters to GB again. Even though he was completely booked all the time, he still found time to write.

> September 3, 1975
>
> I got your nice letter, and I know Paris is a beautiful city. . . .
>
> Today is the 2nd of September and I'm doing the Johnny Carson show tonight. In my next letter I'll tell you how it went. I also did a commercial for Sir Walter

> Raleigh pipe tobacco. The reason they chose me to do
> the commercial is I knew Sir Walter Raleigh personally.
>
> I know that Arlette and Daniel always send you a lot
> of stuff about me. They're sending you the Joyce Haber
> column in the Calendar section of the <u>Times</u>.

The next part of this letter was very upsetting because GB was very close to his sister Goldie and he very rarely mentioned when something was bothering him:

> I'm really writing a lot of nonsense because I don't feel
> too funny. My sister Goldie isn't feeling too well. But
> what can you do? As Dr. Prinzmetal said, "When
> you're old enough you get everything."
>
> I hope you find an apartment very soon. Study hard
> when you go to school so when you come back we'll be
> able to converse in French.
>
> My love to you, and Albin, and Mindy, and Sylvia, and
> Maurice Chevalier.

Every time I wrote to GB it seemed like déjà vu—it was uncomfortably reminiscent of my beginnings in New York. The only difference was that I was now trying to do it in French. GB was very, very busy with his career and still very encouraging about mine, although at this point I was beginning to believe I should find something else to do. Nothing worse than an aging, unemployed blonde!

> September 10, 1975
>
> Now about your birthday on October 12th. I'd like to send you a little money, so write me how I should send it. I'm sending you $300, so do you want it in one check or two? All right, so I spoiled the surprise. When you tell me what to do for your birthday I'll know what to do for Christmas. There, I spoiled the other surprise. I don't know, but I think this year Christmas falls on December 25th. . . .
>
> . . . Keep studying French, Kid, and that goes for Albin, too. Then you can argue in both languages. I forgot, he also knows Spanish so he's one up on you. Well, what the hell, I was one up on you, I could speak Jewish. Poor Lisa, everybody's one up on you. Goodbye, Kid.

Just as I was starting to get my bearings I got the saddest letter from GB. It was this letter that rekindled all my feelings of homesickness. Or was it "GB-sickness"?

September 30, 1975

Well, sad news, my sister Goldie is gone. I went down
there twice. The first time she looked great and I
thought she'd make it, but she didn't. I never knew I
had such a big family. They were all down there. Goldie
was sort of the pivot of my family, she took the place
of my mother, and all the kids, my nieces and
nephews, they all felt that way. They came from all
over--New York, Dallas, even Spain. It was really nice
to see them all, and I'm going to invite them all to my
80th birthday. . . .

. . . This Friday I'm going to New Orleans. I'm being
honored by the National Association of Theater
Owners. I'm the Star of Tomorrow. . . .

. . . In my next letter, which will probably be Monday,
I'll enclose the money order for your birthday. Just
imagine, Lisa, you'll be 27 years old, but to me you'll
always be 18 and running around with that guy,
I forget his name, who played the guitar and had
big feet.

P. S. I get your letters and it's nice to hear from you.

Oh, what a sad letter. GB still had his sister Mamie in New Jersey and his brother Sammy in Akron, but it was Goldie I knew the best.

When I read this letter, I cried and cried. And as I thought about Goldie I remembered all the good stuff she'd taught me and how all she wanted was for me to keep her brother happy. Then I thought of the potato kugel recipe she taught me, and I went out marketing in Paris and came home and made it. Surprisingly enough, I'm still the one who is always responsible for the potato kugel at Passover Seder! Not bad for being "High Goyim." Here's her recipe as I remember it.

Goldie's Potato Kugel

Preheat the oven to 375 degrees.

4 large potatoes
2 eggs
1/2 tsp. baking powder
cooking oil

1 onion
1/2 cup flour
salt and pepper

DIRECTIONS

1. Grate the potatoes. Put the pieces in a bowl of ice water as you grate each one.

2. Brown the chopped onion in a little bit of oil.

3. Remove the potatoes from the ice water and squeeze them out in a towel. (CONTINUED NEXT PAGE)

4. Completely cover the inside of a baking pan with the oil and put it in a 375-degree oven so the oil and the pan get VERY hot--this is the big secret! ! !

5. Lightly beat the eggs, mix with the flour and the baking powder.

6. Mix together the potatoes and the eggs and then pour the egg mixture over it.

7. Make sure the pan in the oven is SIZZLING HOT and pour the mixture into it. This browns the sides and the bottom and makes it crispy.

8. Cook for about forty minutes--azoy! You're ready for Seder!

I was starting to get inconsolably depressed. I was out every day with my modeling portfolio, trying to generate work. Needless to say, I wasn't that successful since I was not one of the great beauties of Paris.

Albin was studying and practicing. I did get to spend time with some of the most famous music teachers and composers in the world, such as Nadia Boulanger. I was encouraged to find that, just as it was with Mme. Lhevinne, the bigger the talent, the humbler the ego. They reminded me very much of GB, and not just because they were all old. Mindy, my cousin, was in art school and very busy every day.

October 7, 1975

I got your nice letter, and it's always good to hear
from you. I'm glad that your French is coming along so
well. All I'm able to say in French is oui-oui, and at my
age even that doesn't come easy. I've got mildewed
shoes to prove it.

I had a wonderful time in New Orleans. Next week I'm
taping the <u>Cher</u> show. Then there's a new variety
show, it's called <u>Saturday Night Live</u>. It's done out of
New York, and I'm doing it with Walter Matthau on
November 1st. Then I'll stay in New York. I'll miss you
kids not having breakfast with me every morning. . . .

. . . Au revoir, or as they say in French, sayonara. I
love you, Kid--and relax.

I finally accepted that the time had come for me to do something about me. So it
was back to school for a teaching credential.

I made this decision while walking along the Seine on a cold, dreary Sunday. I
went home and told Albin and Mindy I needed to go home. But home couldn't be
New York because our apartment was sublet. I knew where home was. I'd always
known where home really was.

The following Wednesday I packed up nine pieces of luggage—including my electric typewriter and Sylvia in her cat carrier—and charged a ticket to Los Angeles. For what I paid in overweight I could have flown first class with unlimited baggage.

The story of my life.

· ELEVEN ·

*"Kid, when you start thinking from
the hips down, you're cooked."*

"G<small>B!</small>"

"Kid! Where are you?"

"I'm at Los Angeles International Airport at TWA."

"Who's with you?"

"Sylvia the cat and all my luggage."

"Daniel'll be right there to get you. Don't move."

I started to cry and for a moment neither of us knew what to say. Then GB continued, "Dinner's in an hour. It'll be good to see you."

Nothing else needed to be said. Sort of like after we burned up the backyard that Fourth of July.

GB didn't ask me very many questions. I told him I wanted to go back to Immaculate Heart and get my teaching credential in English while Albin finished studying. He knew it wasn't true and that I'd had enough of being married, but he didn't get into that. He just told me I could stay as long as I liked. I came to get my credential and stayed for two years.

I called almost no one for awhile because I didn't want to answer any questions and I didn't want to hear what they'd have to say. But I did call Tonda. She had recently had a very nasty

Back from Paris and still playing "Maple Leaf Rag."

breakup with a longtime boyfriend who had turned out to be a really big jerk, and later on turned out to be a really big director and an even bigger jerk, if that was possible!

Tonda and I commiserated and talked about what we were each going to do. She had decided to go back to school and get her master's at UCLA in directing. I was going back to Immaculate Heart. She then told me that our school was in dire financial trouble, threatened to the point that its doors might close for good. We decided that we should, as alums, create a fund-raiser for the school. So together, we produced and directed a musical using students and alums. It consumed the next six months of our lives, but it certainly helped both of us to get through some very rough times and forced us to focus on helping others instead of on our individual problems.

In the midst of putting together this production (Gilbert and Sullivan's *Iolanthe*), I was also back in "GB Land." Our first venture out was to the premiere for *The Sunshine Boys*. GB, Daniel, Arlette, and I went together. The entire evening was like . . . being at a grand Hollywood premiere! None of us that evening had imagined that GB was going to be nominated for an Academy Award.

By Christmas I was ready to let my family and friends know I'd come back. My return had already elicited a number of mixed reactions so I'd inadvertently been through a couple of dress rehearsals dealing with some insensitive off-the-cuff comments. The confrontation that really set the tone and prepared me for what might be in store didn't come from my family at all but from GB's current "friend." Fortunately, it was over the telephone.

One morning, I answered the phone. I was greeted by a female voice demanding, "Who's this?"

"It's Melissa. Who's this?"

"Oh, it's Melissa, now, is it?" After a long pause, she finally asked, "Well, Lisa, what are *you* doing there?"

"I'm living here." By this point I knew who it was and I knew I was hearing genuine panic on her part as she tried to think of what to do about me.

She continued, "So we're back, are we?"

"I don't know about you, but I am."

Now she was truly steamed. "Oh, and we're all grown up with a big mouth . . ."

". . . and sharp teeth to go with it. But you really didn't call to talk to me, did you?" There was the hot silence of frustration so I graciously continued, "GB's at the office. Why don't you try him there? I'll tell him you called just the same."

"Oh, I bet you will."

"If you're going to bet, I just want to tell you the odds will always be in my favor." She hung up.

I don't know what possessed me to be so nasty in what was obviously not an even match. I certainly didn't have the sharp teeth in when I finally called my family members and had to deal with their reactions.

When I went to see my Aunt Noël, cousin Mindy's mother, she was furious. She insinuated that by leaving her daughter alone, living in Paris with my husband, I had probably forced her over the edge into my world of continued "debauchery." Had I known that was the world I was living in, I might have stayed.

My mother said, "Well, it looks like I put that money aside to go to Paris for nothing."

My brothers were my brothers. One said profoundly, "I live on a need-to-know basis, so don't tell me unless I need to know." I think that meant "don't make it my business." My other brother didn't say much since nothing I did surprised him anymore.

With that out of the way, I was ready to start the new year and school. We started the new year by going to the Backus household and then on to a huge party at producer Sam Spiegal's. It was there that I ran into a man I'd met in New York through mutual friends. I'd first met him at my friends' wedding, where he asked me to dance and was very charming. When he introduced himself I recognized his name since he was the director of some very famous, very controversial movies.

He had called me after the wedding and asked to meet with me. I did. He told me he thought he might have a part for me. It didn't take long for me to figure what "part" he meant. And now, here he was at this New Year's party. I excused myself from GB and went over to say hello. He was very surprised, since he thought I was still in Paris, and wanted to know what had happened. I told him about it while we were dancing. After the dance, I left him standing there with a puzzled look on his face as I sat back down next to GB. GB looked at me, looked at the man with whom I'd been dancing, and got the "glint" in his eyes as he looked back at me. "What was that all about?"

I let out a weary sigh. "*Was* is the right word to use."

GB looked me right in the eye and said, "*No* is the right word to use. And you've always been strong about using it."

It looked like GB had the sharp teeth now and he continued, "Behave yourself, Kid, you're not eighteen anymore." I wasn't quite sure what the last part of that statement meant but I knew what the first part meant. So I did.

We settled into a routine: GB going to the office, me going to school during the day and back to school for rehearsals at night, except for Thursday nights when we went out to dinner. The only major interruption was something called The Academy Awards.

GB had been nominated for Best Supporting Actor and had asked me to go with him to the Oscars. I never really liked going to those big public affairs. I found them frightening and I always felt very insecure, but this was so special and I knew I'd have GB to hang on to. Every time we'd talk about it, I asked him if deep down inside he thought he might win and he'd answer, "Who the hell knows? If I do, it will only be because I'm so goddam old!" As we all know, he did win and it wasn't because he was old. It was because he was good. And he only got better.

Going to the Academy Awards with manager Irving Fein.

His next movie, *Oh, God!*, became my favorite. He makes so many observations in it that seem to reflect the essence of his own philosophy of life. While he was filming this, we didn't see too much of one another. Tonda and I were deep into production for

Iolanthe and I was preparing to go back to New York and face Albin. Earlier in the year, he and I had finally admitted that it was not working. It was nobody's fault, but we just didn't belong together.

GB never asked me what I was going to do when I got to New York. He just told me to take care of myself and remember that "you're not easy and Albin's a nice fella."

All of that may have been true but it didn't help matters when I got to New York.

We tried to settle things amicably. But everything escalated rapidly to a fever pitch; I did my usual and finally just bailed.

I arrived home July 3rd unannounced. Needless to say, GB was surprised to see me, but delighted. He could tell that what transpired with Albin had not been anything resembling a reconciliation. He could tell that I was angry and upset and just about anything he was going to say to me about me and marriage was not going to be appreciated. I got something to drink and plopped down across from him to wait for dinner.

Finally, he did a slow take that included a sip of his martini and a puff of his cigar followed by a very slow exhale. "Well, I guess you won't be wanting any fireworks for tomorrow since you look like you've had your fill."

I didn't have a comeback so he continued, "Look, you've still got Sylvia, you've got school, you've got your friends, you've got hot soup coming up, and you'll always have me." I went and threw my arms around his neck and hugged him as hard as I'd ever hugged anyone.

"Kid, not so hard. Remember, I'm booked."

And that was the end of that.

·TWELVE·

*"What're you trying to do, Kid,
teach yourself a lesson?"*

GB thought that since I wasn't going to stay married, I should try and get back into show business. He said he had an agent for me. I couldn't say no because I knew he'd say, "What else are you doing for the summer?" I met the agent and she immediately had calls for me to go on that didn't interest me. She also had a singing teacher for me, who taught opera, of all things. I told GB if I could learn to sing opera I could do anything. Then it was back to the musical theater workshop. This time, because my entrance had been prefaced with a call from GB's office, my reception was much different than the first had been. But that didn't change things from my perspective. It was still a group of people who talked more about working than actually worked and who knew more about show business than the people working in it did.

It was also back to dance classes. That was one part I really liked, so that was okay.

As the summer was coming to an end and it was time to get back to school, GB suggested that I take the next semester off and concentrate on all the other things I had going. I agreed, but I also took a "regular job" running the office of a friend from college.

I now had plenty to do but that didn't last too long. GB put an end to my "regular job" by offering me a job on his upcoming special, in a WWI production number featuring Walter Matthau with eight tap dancers backing him up. It really was fun: I loved the rehearsals and I loved actually getting paid for tap dancing, which is something I'd do for free. Also on the show was a popular young actress who was to do one of the Burns and Allen routines with GB. He kept asking me how I felt about it. I thought she was very funny, but that wasn't what he wanted to hear. He finally reminded me that it could be me. I reminded him that I was perfectly happy dancing in the chorus. Besides, I got her beautiful dress after it was all over.

This dress showed up hanging in the butler's pantry one day when I came home. I knew all about the dress. The actress had been given a clothing budget of so much and had gone *way* over it by getting this dress. It was a gypsy dress out of painted chiffon, gold brocade, ribbons, beading, and embroidery with a huge full skirt and very low neckline. Not only had she gone way over budget, but she had the costume department alter it so it couldn't be returned and probably wouldn't fit anyone else anyway. I guess she figured this way they would let her keep it even after what she'd done. Boy, was she ever wrong. Her behavior made GB really angry, so he didn't let her keep the dress and as an afterthought brought it home to me. It fit perfectly.

Me in the gypsy dress.

I wore it that New Year's to all the parties we went to and wherever we went it got a lot of attention. First we went to the Backuses as usual. From there we went to Grace and Harold Robbins's party at Gatsby's and had our dinner and danced. It still wasn't midnight but GB had had enough and asked me what other parties there might be. I did know of one party to which we'd been invited but really had never thought we'd make. But that's exactly where we ended up: at a party at my friend Stephen's house.

Stephen had been my master teacher while I was student teaching and he'd met GB during this time. And Stephen and I had mutual friends, including Tonda, who I knew would be there, too.

When GB and I arrived, I must say it did cause a brief stir. GB has always been a "good mixer." Tonda came over to chat and point out to us the fella she had been but was no longer seeing. Right after that he came over and introduced himself. He said he was Paul Berry and GB said, "Why don't you sit down, Kid?" And he and GB chatted for the rest of the evening. They talked about Orrey Kelly, who had been a great friend of Gracie's, and Cary Grant when he was "Archibald Leach" and roommates with Orrey Kelly and the two of them had sold hand-painted ties. GB told some stories that I hadn't heard in years and I could tell that he was finally having a good time. That was not the last time we were to see Paul.

Several months after this, GB decided that I should do some things around the house to freshen it up. Other than the bedroom renovation, it had been nearly ten years since I'd done anything like this. Unfortunately, the only thing I disliked more than shopping was shopping for the house. He reminded me that the fella we'd met at Stephen's had an interior design business, so he suggested that I call him. Tonda gave me the number and I set up an appointment for us to meet with Paul.

Paul and GB hit it off again when Paul suggested that maybe the house should be restored to the way it looked in the '30s when Gracie first had it done: beautiful antiques, fabrics, and designed for maximum comfort. Since then, it had slowly come to resemble nothing even close to this concept. GB thought for a minute while I rooted around in a nearby cupboard and found some 1930's photographs of the rooms. They looked just as Paul had described and GB loved the idea. The only drawback for me was that, as nice as Paul was, I was relegated to be the intermediary on the project. Yuk! Furniture, fabrics, and the end of any free time I had since I was now teaching several days a week.

Paul made the whole thing very painless with his easy professionalism, unwavering sense of style, and unflinching tolerance of me. It seemed that no matter what was brought for GB's final approval, GB loved it. Eventually I was eliminated from those final approval meetings, which was fine by me. But there was one morning in particular, after a grueling date, when it certainly wasn't so fine by me.

I came downstairs that morning not knowing that Paul was there for a meeting. Paul and GB were having coffee in the breakfast room and discussing what to do with the living room and the summer porch.

Since my divorce from Albin, I'd been dating an old friend from college. He had never been very nice to me and it was evident that he only wanted to go out with me because he was a bit star-struck around GB. GB was on to this, too, but rather than tell me, he figured he'd let me use the discovery method. It gave him something new to give me a hard time about when I was being a pain in the neck.

I'd been out with this guy the night before and once again was frustrated and had cried myself to sleep. I came downstairs by way of the back stairs and didn't realize that anyone was in the breakfast room. I got myself a cup of coffee and swung open the door and there were GB and Paul, all fresh and crispy very early in the morning, and there I was: Mascara was all over my face, my hair looked like a long blond rat's nest, and I had on an old pale lavender ratty tatty Barbara Stanwyck–like chenille bathrobe with a huge peacock on the back.

GB and Paul both looked at me as I stood there, frozen and mortified. After a beat GB looked at Paul, Paul looked back at him, and they both returned to looking at me, whereupon GB said sarcastically, "Nice outfit, Kid. Why don't you sit down and join us?"

As I sheepishly sat down, GB continued, "Out with 'the fella' again, huh, Kid?" And then, *What are you trying to do? Teach yourself a lesson?*

Suddenly, I realized what GB was saying to me and he was right! I had everything in the world going for me and there I was, shooting myself in the foot.

I looked at Paul, who, six years later, became my second husband. He smiled and shrugged and we all just started laughing, and they resumed their talk about redoing the house.

It was during this spring that GB suggested I should have a ladies' luncheon at Hillcrest for all my girlfriends. He said he thought it might be fun since not everyone thought of Hillcrest as their own personal dining room. I invited seven of my girlfriends, most of whom I'd met at Immaculate Heart.

We met at the house first, and went over together. GB had gotten us a big round table right up front and was sitting there waiting for us. We all sat down and I introduced him to anyone I thought he might have forgotten. After these introductions, he told us all to order ourselves drinks and asked the waiter for menus. I knew why he continued to sit with us after the menus came. He wanted to see what we were going to eat because he had his own ideas about it. He was big on the minute steak; chopped salad; matzo, eggs, and onions (remember that?); or broiled whitefish. The menu offered myriad choices, and in spite of what he thought, some of those present had been to Hillcrest before. In fact, a couple of them were even Jewish! But that didn't make any difference to him. He had to be in on the suggesting and ordering.

Tonda saw that there was a tongue sandwich on the menu, and with great enthusiasm said that was certainly what she intended to have! One of the girls sitting across the table threw her head up from her menu with great alarm and asked Tonda in a shocked voice, "A tongue sandwich? My God! How can you eat something that comes from an animal's mouth?" No one knew quite how to respond, except for GB, who took a slug of Bloody Mary (those had replaced lunchtime martinis after the heart surgery), looked across the table, and exclaimed, "Yeah, how can you eat something that comes from an animal's mouth? Have an egg instead!"

With that he excused himself and went into the other dining room. We sat there, stunned. I think after that a few of us reserved our cravings for tongue sandwiches, sautéed brains, and perhaps liver and onions for that occasional dinner at Musso and Frank.

GB was very, very busy working and very, very happy. He felt like he was really back in show business. The frosting on his cake, so to speak, was all the requests to make more records. He'd always loved to sing. Even though he knew he didn't have a great voice, he knew he had a great delivery. He was being courted with offers for country-western albums, best-of albums, duet albums, concert albums. There was one time before dinner when we were chatting about this and I was trying to get him to admit that he loved all the recording offers.

"Come on, GB, you've waited so long. You know you love it. You never expected this at your age." Then I went through all the possibilities that had been offered: "You never expected *George Burns Goes Nashville, George Burns Goes Broadway, George Burns Goes Hollywood.*"

"You're right, Kid, I guess the only thing I expected at my age was *George Burns Goes Soft.*"

I shook my head in mock despair. And changed the subject to an upcoming event and subsequent request that I had.

Arlette and Daniel were anxiously awaiting the arrival of their baby. I wanted to give Arlette a baby shower at Butterfield's, and I wanted GB to sponsor it. After the lunch at Hillcrest, he asked, how could he refuse?

Arlette gave me a guest list that included several friends of mine. I called the restaurant and arranged for the menu and the wine. That was the big mistake on my part—not only on the phone but later at the restaurant.

It was a lovely Saturday afternoon and we had a small private dining room. There were probably a dozen of us. I'm sure that it was my friends who drank most of the wine because we ended up skinny-dipping at GB's at four in the afternoon.

It started out as a very proper shower with luncheon, gifts, jokes, and everyone having a good time. But by the time the check came (so I've been told) I'd flashed my tube top at the waiter and we'd gone through a case of wine. The next thing I knew, three of us were accosting GB in the summer porch at home where he was watching the news and having a cocktail. We were really on a roll. We decided swimming was the next thing and tried to convince GB to join us. Of course, he said no, and with that we all started stripping off our clothes as he called for Daniel. As I remember, Daniel came in, took one look, and decided to go back into the kitchen to get fresh ice for the ice bucket.

Before we knew it, we'd stripped down to our panties and were racing and screaming around the summer porch, laughing hysterically. GB had never seen anything like it and sat there helpless. I led everyone to the door leading to the yard and pool and suggested that we race the length of the yard and end by jumping in the pool.

GB diplomatically tried to dissuade such antics but we were already rushing toward the pool. We all dived in with a huge splash and started screaming and laughing and scrambled out to do it again! GB was trying to reason with each of us individually as we raced back to the house. Suddenly, I came up with a brilliant idea: GB should join us! We beckoned him toward the pool. He yelled for Daniel, who responded immediately but screeched to a halt when he saw the scene in the backyard: three very drunk, topless women in their late twenties dragging poor GB toward the pool.

Daniel rescued GB, and the two of them hurried back into the house and let us exhaust ourselves laughing, screaming, and yelling.

The next thing I remembered was being up in my bathroom, very wet and wishing I were dead. But not as much as I did the next morning.

I came cringing downstairs to breakfast. GB eyed me over the top of his newspaper. I'd never really gotten into serious trouble with him in all our years together, and I had the feeling this was to be the first time. He watched me gingerly sit down and pour myself some coffee. There was an enormous silence. Finally, he spoke.

"I guess you kids had a good time for yourselves."

I just looked at him.

As he returned to his paper he said to no one in particular, "You're not easy but you're all I've got." What a guy! (What a hangover!)

Earlier in the spring I'd decided to study at the Royal Academy of Dramatic Arts in London for the summer. GB was very busy so it was fine with him. In fact, he was going over to London to do *The Muppet Show,* so we could go together. And we did.

We first checked into the Inn on the Park. It certainly wasn't anything like the Dorchester where we'd stayed during our previous trek to London. GB tried to convince me that the Dorchester just wasn't the same as it used to be. But I don't know how much odder than this hotel it could have gotten. We occupied a suite; the entire rest of the floor was occupied by the Queen of Qatar. There were guards all over. We were scrutinized every time we got off the elevator, where we were greeted by the smell of some very strange food being prepared. It seemed that "she" did not eat anything from the kitchen and had a full staff with her.

What a difference ten years can make.

Before GB had to get to work and I had to get to school, we went back to Brighton Beach and Brighton Pavillion. We ate our lunch in the same restaurant we had in December of '69. We found the same theater where he and Gracie had played and we had the same good time that we'd had before. Then it was time to get to work.

I'd found a room in a boarding house near RADA so I could walk to school every day. I knew it was nothing that GB would have chosen for himself, but it was what I could afford. He insisted on going there and to RADA before he left to see what I was getting myself into. The quaint rooming house made him smile. Then we walked the few blocks to RADA and went inside. It was an old, dreary, multistory building. GB wanted to look around, though the girl at the desk didn't seem too sure about us Americans. But she acquiesced and as we walked away someone recognized him and the place was buzzing.

He knew that I didn't want anyone there to know who I knew. That I wanted to be just another student. He smiled at me apologetically as we left. I smiled back. He never needed to apologize to me for anything. Not then—not ever.

It was a very bittersweet parting, for I had decided that after this summer I was going to move out of GB's house. I'd gotten the independence bug again. Before we'd left Los Angeles I'd found an apartment near to where I was going to be teaching and was set to move on September 1. The change wasn't as bad this time as it had been the first.

Notice the Oscar, plus the photos of us on the mantel.

This time GB was very busy and not so dependent on me for companionship as he had been the first time. I was only going to be living about two miles away from him. And he still had Ramona the cat, so I was going to take Sylvia with me.

That summer at RADA was, as they say, the "final curtain" for my life as a performer. On a daily basis I realized I just wasn't driven. Everyone around me was so ambitious and obsessed with having a career regardless of their degree of talent. They worked so hard during our eight-hour days and spent the evenings and weekends going to as much theater as they could afford. I spent my evenings reading but not really going over my work. I spent the weekends going out dining and gambling with one of the Muppets.

No, my heart wasn't in it. After I got home that summer I never took another singing lesson, never went on another audition, and never worked as a performer again.

·THIRTEEN·

"Kid, just make it like we're
schmoozing so the words fit
my mouth."

When I moved out that fall, it really didn't change things that much. I was teaching every day and GB was busy with different projects. A couple of times a week, in addition to our usual Thursdays, I'd have dinner at the house and then go back to my place and correct papers for the next day.

My new place needed some attention and Paul said he'd help with some suggestions to make it more comfortable. I was all for that! I still didn't care about paint and fabric although I did like things to be "together." I had some furniture from GB's house that needed to be reupholstered and Paul guaranteed me that if I'd only look at fabrics for one day, he'd get the rest of the work done.

One afternoon, Paul and I went shopping to all the places I'd gone for GB's house. I feared that it was all going to be way out of my budget. In the second store we visited, as Paul was flipping through fabrics, he flashed past one that was perfect. I made him stop and go back to it. I really liked it, and when he found out the price, I figured I could afford it. I gave him the green light. He looked at me in astonishment for a moment and then fell to the floor with a thud. Here was this tall, handsome, self-assured businessman prone at my feet! I stared at him not knowing what to do or say. Then he looked up at me and said, "I've never had anyone make such a firm decision about anything so fast." I should have told him he'd never heard me say no, but I didn't have the presence of mind.

He got up laughing and dusting himself off and I realized for the first time how utterly charming and spontaneous he was. But uh-oh—madness lay ahead. And it was my own.

Because Paul had offered me his sources at his price to help me get the apartment together, he'd stop by to check its progress. He was always nonplussed and positive about what was going on. While I'd be there in a foul mood grading papers after having taught nearly two hundred students during the day, he'd swing by and revive my dreary mood with his energetic, positive, good-guy manner.

Eventually, we went out for dinner. I told GB about going out with him and his comment was, "Why not, Kid? He's a nice man. Besides, he's tall and doing well." Those were never exactly my criteria for dating, but if GB approved I figured I should probably listen.

Paul and I started seeing more and more of one another although my old "friend" from college was still around. That wasn't a problem. He actually hired Paul to put his new house in shape. I finally accepted there was no future there.

In November of that year, I invited Paul to go to my mother's house up north for a long weekend. We didn't tell GB. I don't know exactly why. GB liked and respected Paul, and he and I both knew we were a "two act" no matter what was ever to pass. But even though he was eighty-one, he was a man and he did have an ego.

As Paul and I drove to Burbank Airport we passed Warner Bros. and the billboard "du jour" in front of the studio. It was the *Oh, God!* poster, in which GB was holding up a finger in a "listen to me" gesture. We both looked at each other. Paul, knowing that I hadn't been honest with GB, waited for my reaction.

All I could say was, "Oh dear." It was another fine mess I'd gotten myself into.

■ ■ ■ ■ ■ ■ ■ ■ ■ ■ ■ ■ ■ ■

By the end of that year, with the death of Packy (Elon Packard), it seemed that GB had lost most of his writers in a short period of time. This wasn't a good thing for more reasons than one. He was deep into one of the many books he was to write. He half-jokingly asked me to write something for him as a sample because he was pretty sure I could come work for him and get the job done. Besides that, he *needed* me to come write for him. Why? Because I was the only other person who knew all his stories and that was the only way he could finish the book. Or so he said.

The following excerpts are from the sample chapter I wrote in 1977. GB asked me to quit teaching school and come work for him. As he put it to me then, "Just write something up, Kid, so I can see if you can make the words fit my mouth." You know what? I knew just what he meant! I had to be able to write in a manner that sounded as if someone was just schmoozing.

WINTER 1976

Well, I'm back. I don't know whether you remember me or not from the chapter about me in GB's last book, so if you don't you can refer to pages 199–211 in Living It Up (Or, They Still Love Me in Altoona). *When GB finished writing the chapter about me I was still living in Paris. That didn't last too long. I came back to Los Angeles and GB's house until I could find a place of my own. It's been two years now and I'm still looking.*

The first thing GB wanted me to do when I came into town was to read the rough draft of the book he had just written—in particular the chapter he'd written about knowing me. Well, the information in this chapter wasn't exactly how I remembered things. Don't get me wrong. It's a good chapter and it's very funny but you know how he lies. When he asked me if I liked the stuff about me, I had to tell him the truth: It was awfully funny but it made me look awfully goofy and I didn't think that was fair. You see, he's every bit as goofy as I am. I thought the chapter should have mentioned some of the goofy things he had done when I was around.

When I told GB this, he got that funny glint in his eyes that he gets when he thinks you're being unnecessarily "jerky" (his word). He told me if he ever wrote another book he would have me write a chapter so I could show everyone how smart I am. I could see that he didn't understand.

It wasn't that I didn't like what he had written; it was just that it made me look so silly and him so smart. So, now that he had challenged me I had to say that I would, of course, be more than happy to write a chapter for his new book—that is, if they ever asked him to write another book. I told him it would be a pleasure to let everyone know the "truth." Finally I told him that anyone can write the truth and still hold the interest of the reader. Getting a college degree had made me very adept at putting my foot in my mouth. In fact, I was almost double-jointed.

Wouldn't you know it?—GB was asked to write another book. And wouldn't you know that GB hadn't forgotten our previous conversation. I was hoping that if I didn't mention it, we could both gracefully forget about the whole conversation. But that's not what happened. He told me he was starting the next book and wondered when would I have my material ready to turn in to him. The final word on it was, "It had better be funny, too." If it weren't, he'd make it funny. I knew then I was in deep trouble.

Now, the path of defeat was right in front of me, but that's as useless as the path of righteousness, and I'd never given in to either one. I knew that GB expected me to not take him up on his offer because I'm not a writer. I mean, I'd written plenty of college research papers on Elizabethan Theater and the true meaning of Hamlet, *but funny stuff had not been my forte. That was GB's job, not mine. So I knew this was going to be hard. Real hard.*

I sat around sharpening my pencils and wondering, How hard could it be?

There are plenty of people who write funny stuff every day. I even know some of them. It's just that I'm not one of them. I finally decided on a plan. I would hang out at GB's office and see how he writes all his funny stuff. He's a good writer so I knew I would pick up some techniques.

And I did. The best one was to hire myself a writer. After all, he has Jack Langdon and Elon Packard to help bounce around ideas. I needed someone to bounce ideas around with, someone to tell me I was going in the right direction. I needed Woody Allen. That was the answer. I would write to Woody Allen and ask him to help me write this chapter. Just the week before, GB and I had seen his latest movie, Annie Hall, *and GB thought it was one of the all-time great movies. Woody Allen was the perfect choice.*

When I told my girlfriend about all this, she suggested that when I write to Woody, I should not only offer money but some added attractions. It was such a good suggestion that I almost asked her *to write my chapter. But anyway, I started to compose the letter. I knew I had to make the offer very attractive. I would not only offer him money but he could come and live in my room at GB's house while he was writing the chapter and I would stay in the spare room. He could even use all of my things, including my electric typewriter and my telephone with the answering service. He could use the swimming pool and get a little color. And lastly, we would all eat together. I was sure these temptations would convince him this was the best job offer he'd had in years.*

Of course, during all of this, ol' Woody and I would sit in my room and exchange witty thoughts (mostly his) and he would find angles on all my stories about GB's goofiness, and GB would think I was terribly clever to get a writer of my own, and such a good one at that! Finally, this would mean that the chapter would be terrific. It was a brilliant idea. All I had to do was write the perfect letter. Right around here, I remembered I wasn't a writer.

I called my friend Tonda Marton ("The Scholar") and told her the idea, thinking she would help me to write this perfect letter. Her enthusiasm did not match mine. In fact, she thought it was a very odd idea. "Woody Allen is a very busy person," she said. "Where are you going to get the money to pay him?" She also thought he would be insulted.

I went along with the first two arguments but I didn't think he would be insulted. In fact, I know he would have done it . . . if I had asked him. What an opportunity he missed!

So I didn't write the letter and now I must write this chapter by myself. Okay. Now that I've proven to you that I'm probably as goofy as GB made me out to be in his first book, I'm going to prove to you that he is every bit as goofy as I am. (You know the old saying, "Takes one to know one!") Why did I say that? It's

not funny at all . . . oh well. I think the best place to start would be with the dis-
aster stories—those situations that would have had disastrous endings—had I
not been there.

Honest.

I thought what I had written as the opening to my chapter was very clever and funny. GB thought it was silly. I continued writing my sample chapter, maintaining the premise that he was goofy. Here are a couple of the "goofy" examples that now, twenty years later, don't seem so "goofy" at all.

It was a very quiet morning. Daniel and Arlette—see photo in Living It Up (Or, They Still Love Me in Altoona)*—who run GB's house, were off for the day, the cats were outside beating up other cats, I was in my room studying, and GB was getting ready to go to his office. GB came into my room, teased me for about three minutes, asked what I wanted for dinner, and then left for the office. Not funny, huh? Well, it gets better.*

Five minutes later I smelled smoke. Not just the smoke of an El Producto cigar but the smoke of something burning. Like a house. I ran out into the hall and saw a finger of smoke drifting from under the door of GB's room.

Hesitantly, I opened the door. The room was not only filling with smoke, but there were flames in his dressing room. I grabbed some towels from the bathroom and turned on the faucets and put out the fire. I don't know whether I beat it to death or drowned it but it was out. I know, I know, I should have called the fire department, but I just didn't. As I looked around the dressing room I could see how the fire had started. Maybe you've already guessed it. His cigar. When GB lights his cigar he often doesn't blow out the match but merely throws the lit match into the ashtray to go out by itself. Well, that's exactly what he had done this morning and the match lit the paper wrapper from his cigar, and the paper lit the hand towel, and the hand towel lit the wallpaper, and there went the dressing room.

I immediately called the office but he wasn't too interested. I guess either he was writing or he had Trixie Hicks there because all he said was, "Good for you, Kid," and he was sorry it had happened, and he would see me at dinner. The finish of this story is that he still doesn't blow out his matches after he lights his cigars. I know this isn't a funny finish but at least it's the truth.

Maybe it's time to move on from the disaster stories to those stories that involve other people who have witnessed GB at his goofiest. There is one story with approximately two hundred witnesses but I won't mention their names because I want to make it short. You probably won't fall down laughing but you might get a small chuckle out of it.

GB, his son Ronnie, and I went to San Diego for the bar mitzvah of GB's sister Goldie's grandson. (Yes, there really is a Goldie.) We arrived on a Friday night, met everyone, and got the directions to the temple for the next day.

The following morning, bright and early, the three of us were off to the bar mitzvah, and we arrived just as things were beginning to get under way. Very quietly, although I've found out that bar mitzvahs aren't so quiet, we went in and took our seats. As we sat there and looked around we didn't see anyone we knew. Not a soul. But everyone sure was looking at us. I looked at the bar mitzvah boy and finally whispered to GB, "I didn't know that Billy looked like that." GB whispered back, "Neither did I." You guessed it! We were at the wrong temple, wrong bar mitzvah! Very quietly, even more so than when we came in, we headed for the car. Eventually we found the right temple, went in very quietly, and started nodding hello again—only this time to the right people.

I don't think GB seems very goofy from these stories. If only I could have gotten Woody. He knows all about bar mitzvahs and could have made that last story very funny.

I think that wraps it up for now. There are some other stories but unless I can get Woody to help me out . . . I just can't do it. There is one more thing I can add without Woody's help. I love GB very, very much in spite of and because of his goofiness. He is one of the nicest men I'll ever know. Why am I so sure of this? Became he's always telling me that he's the nicest man I'll ever meet. And you know what? For once he's telling the truth.

He liked it! I got the job.

·FOURTEEN·

"Kid, it was only stuff."

"Yeah, but GB, it was my *stuff!"*

I quit my job teaching English and became one of GB's writers.

Being one of his writers had all sorts of ramifications. First of all, the guys in the office knew that GB and I had been the "closest" of friends for years. And we all knew that he hired me because it was a good way to see me every day. I knew it and they knew it, but once again I really didn't care what everyone else thought. At $300 a week for two hours of work a day I knew it was a gravy train job, and biscuit tires had been thrown in! I also knew deep down inside that there was something there for me to experience. I didn't quite know what, but GB always exuded such strength and positiveness when he was talking show biz that there was an electric charge around him during these times. His innate sense of what worked and what didn't was very attractive and somehow comforting.

So there I was, after twelve years, back with GB every day. And loving it. I lived nearby and used to ride my bike to work, always arriving about ten minutes before GB. The "guys" were always sitting around schmoozing and rarely included me, which

Working in the office with GB and writers Fred Fox, Hasl Goldman, and Seaman Jacobs.

was fine because I always brought my knitting and kept myself occupied. But I do remember one time when I arrived slightly winded wearing my usual shorts and T-shirt, one of the writers blatantly looked at my heaving bosom and made a lewd comment about, of all things, my nipples! I let him finish with his observations while all the other guys laughed. I could hear GB walking down the hall toward the office and with perfect timing I informed this writer that as soon as he got "off my back," he could "kiss my ass!" With this, GB naively came in and we went to work. It wasn't always easy being in the office.

Thankfully, it wasn't the other writers that made the various aspects of the job so interesting. It always returned to GB's take on work. So self-assured, confident, strict, and *always* unruffled no matter what the situation was.

One morning, we were in the middle of rewrites for yet another one of GB's upcoming films when suddenly there was an enormous crash next to my chair and the nose of a '69 Chevy came through the wall and parked itself. Unnerving? To myself and the other writers it was. To GB . . . no. We were working so he got up and moved to the other side of the room and continued to discuss the possible script changes. What had happened? Nothing so very complicated. The old General Service Studios on Las Palmas Avenue (later to become Zoetrope Studios and then something else) had offices that backed up to an alley, and GB had a suite of these offices. Two very drunk fellas went to turn into the alley, miscalculated the turn, and ended up with us. We continued working while the men tried to figure out how to extract the car from the building. And, at noon, GB went to Hillcrest for his broiled tail of whitefish and a martini and I got on my bike and went home.

It was during this time when we had all the scripts coming in that I realized how unfamiliar I was with the screenplay form and that I'd better smarten up.

I enrolled in a screenplay writing course. The course required that I write an original screenplay using the paradigm I was being taught. So I did. It was about (guess what?) a successful, charmingly stubborn, randy old man; his son, who returns to live with him and go to college; and the girl who the son meets and what happens among all of them. It was originally entitled *Keep It Warm for Me* but as the script developed so did the characters; I changed the title to *No Free Lunch*.

GB was very enthusiastic. More than the screenplay, he loved the fact that every afternoon I went home and worked. With my newfound knowledge, I felt justified in accepting screen credit along with the other writers in the office for the latest script out of the office: *Oh, God! Book II.*

It was a very enlightening experience for me the few times I went to the set. I watched the director take what we had envisioned as a sweet movie and, with the sensibility of a Talmudic scholar, weigh it down with meaning that wasn't there.

When I was introduced to the various people on the set, I was met with the same attitude as ten years earlier when GB had first started taking me out and introducing me to his friends. I was tolerated because GB was powerful and his attitude was basically "love me—love my dog." Ten years earlier I'd been a harmless puppy, but now I was a full-grown dog and someone to be wary of since my position was unclear. I suppose I could have made a few of the more arrogant people I met temporarily miserable if I'd chosen. I couldn't be bothered. Besides, bitchy behavior on my part would have made GB look bad.

The credits went into arbitration at the Writers Guild because the man who wrote the original screenplay protested our screen credits. By getting a screen credit I was now a member of the Writers Guild, which opened a whole other world to me. I became active on the Publications Committee and then the Women's Committee. Through the women on the Women's Committee I learned about an organization called Women in Film and applied for membership with the sponsorship of two of the women from the committee. All of this new involvement certainly came at just the right time because GB was constantly in and out of town filming and giving concerts, so the office was pretty quiet.

Early on during all this, Paul and I had started living together. Oddly enough, the place we got was the very same apartment where GB and I had gone to the New Year's party and met Paul for the first time. Although GB knew I was seeing Paul, it did take some time for me to tell him that we were now living together. I remember hinting at it more and more every week at dinner until eventually it was out in the open and that was that. Now, instead of GB inviting *me* places, he invited *us*. And likewise, when

Paul and I threw parties we always included GB. We also brought GB to parties at Paul's clients' houses. GB always seemed to like meeting new people, and these affairs certainly always gave him a new audience. Sometimes I doubted whether he really wanted to go or just felt that it was good for him to get out of the house when he wasn't working, but it never seemed an important enough question to pose.

Paul, GB, and me.

In the fall of '82, right after Paul and I had returned from a lengthy vacation, I was offered a book to write. It was for a workout book featuring this real character from Brooklyn who had created this workout guru persona and had recently ingratiated himself to just about everyone in Hollywood. What they wanted was a fitness book that was serious yet sounded like him and with his sense of humor. I accepted, and for the next year and a half I worked on it, including the book production. It was a real education in many ways. I would go to GB and tell him what was going on and how frustrating it was and he'd say, "Stick with it, Kid, you might learn something." Besides learning about the publishing business, I learned that contracts are made to be broken and that when people begin to believe their own PR, hope for the best and expect the worst! (I also realized that this philosophy could apply to marriage as Paul and I married in 1983.)

I must have done an acceptable job because Simon & Schuster immediately offered me another book. Same sort of thing but completely different "main character." Thank God! I delivered this book just in time to deliver our first son, Nathaniel.

We'd spent a great deal of time trying to find a name we liked since the last name Berry was so common. We decided that family names were always a good solution, and since we considered GB family and Nathan was a fine name, that's what we went with. Also, no one else had named any of their children after GB and it seemed like a nice thing to do. But some friends of ours told us there was a problem with this: In the Jewish religion it's not acceptable to name someone after someone who's still living. Nathan Birnbaum was certainly still living—so Nathan Berry became Nathaniel Berry!

Our new routine now included dragging baby gear to GB's for our weekly dinner.

GB and godson Nathaniel poolside.

GB would hold Nathaniel (and later his brother Ben) on his lap, stick his finger in his martini, and pop it in Nathaniel's mouth, who would smack his baby lips approvingly. This became a tradition that was to be upheld for the next eleven years.

That Father's Day, when we went to GB's for a visit, we found him sitting stiffly in the summer porch, having a cup of tea. Before anyone could say anything, he blurted out that Ramona the cat was dead. I'd never, ever seen him so forlorn. He looked down at his hands folded in his lap and started to cry. We sat down with him, not knowing what to say. I softly promised him that I'd go the next day and get another kitty that looked just the same, even though we all knew that it was impossible to replace poor ol' Ramona.

The next day I went out and bought him another Seal Point Himalayan and another Blue Point Himalayan that looked like Eli even though Eli had been gone a long time. He named the Seal Point Jolie after Al Jolsen because, as he told me, "they both work in blackface makeup!" He looked like a little boy at Christmas with his new kittens wobbling around on the table in front of him.

We continued to have our weekly dinners, between which GB was usually out of town working. We'd bought a house into which I was putting lots of time and energy; I was also working on various freelance jobs. Paul's business had expanded to the East Coast, so he was traveling

We were never sure what Poppa was going to give Baby Ben a taste of—the bottle, the gin martini, or the cigar!

as well. On a trip to visit some of Paul's new clients, something truly devastating happened that we were going to have to tell GB.

In the fall of 1989, Paul and I were invited to be houseguests of some clients of his in the south of France. Since everything was status quo on the homefront—with everyone in good health and happy, including GB and our new son, Benjamin—we accepted the invitation.

We arrived in Cap d'Antibes from Italy very late in the afternoon and had to hustle to make it downstairs in time for dinner. While we were downstairs having dinner, someone in the household staff came into our room and very methodically went through all my jewelry. I couldn't believe it when I realized what had happened the next morning. As I tearfully went through everything—discovering more and more items missing—I realized that what was taken amounted to a considerable sum of money. GB had always reminded me that the jewelry he had given me was basically "money in the bank." Well, not anymore. And much worse than that, it all had a great sentimental value since all of it had either belonged to Gracie or had been in my family or been given to me by Paul.

Paul's clients took no responsibility for the robbery and said that the burglars must have been "gypsies who came by way of the sea." They also took *no* financial responsibility for any of my things, and my insurance covered very little of it.

I knew I would have to come home and tell GB what had happened. I was terrified. He'd repeatedly told me (since 1973) to be careful; I always had been and had most of the jewelry for over twenty years without a problem. To complicate the situation, GB knew these people and had gone with us to their house for dinner many times. And he had entertained them in return.

When we got home, I told Paul I needed to go to GB's alone for dinner. He knew why. I hadn't seen GB since we'd returned, so he was surprised that I arrived without any of my family. As he looked at me, he knew something wasn't right. I finally got the courage to explain what had happened. He just shook his head like he always did, told me not to cry, and said, "Kid, it's only stuff!"

"Yeah, GB, but it was *my* stuff!"

"Well, they're short people in a house that's too big for them and now we don't have to go there and eat their fancy food anymore!"

"If you felt that way, why did you ever go there with us in the first place?"

"I thought it would help Paul's business."

He always seemed to find the up side of a bad situation!

Soon after this, I realized that, in some instances, continuing to socialize with Paul's clients was emotionally and mentally unhealthy for me and for my marriage. This decision did exacerbate some serious problems that Paul and I were beginning to have. But I knew that to continue a lifestyle of excess and hypocrisy of which I'd been a part was going to render me useless as a human being and therefore not any good to anyone else.

What would return a sense of balance and order to my unraveling life? What would make me feel that I was useful and that I was using my education for something besides planning dinner parties? Teaching. I'd always liked teaching English. I'd always liked being with teachers.

On a whim, I looked in the classified section of the paper under "Teachers." There was a mornings-only position in language arts in a local Catholic middle school for which I'd be perfectly suited. That meant I would still have afternoons for whatever I needed to do—which still included running the house, freelance writing, and picking children up from school.

I went for the interview that afternoon and started work the following Monday. What a relief to be with real, caring people with real values in a nurturing environment where the focus was on how much one could give rather than how much one could acquire.

It was this radical rethinking of my goals and change of environment that gave me the strength to get through what lay ahead of me both in my marriage and with GB.

·FIFTEEN·

*"I'm not saying yes or no, I'm
staying five more years."*

When the phone rang that summer morning of 1994 and I heard Daniel's voice, I assumed it was the usual weekly call to confirm that I'd be there for dinner. It wasn't. Daniel very gently told me that there had been an accident, and although GB was all right now, he needed some time to rest so I shouldn't come for dinner. Naturally I wanted to know about the accident.

Daniel downplayed the fall GB had taken to assuage my fears, but in fact GB had cracked his skull. I called every day to see how he was doing and to find out when I could come see him. Finally, Daniel told me that GB wasn't doing so well. He seemed to be having short-term memory loss and some speech impairments, and was getting ready to go back and have some tests that would require a stay in the hospital. I asked if I could come see him right away before he went to the doctor, and Daniel said yes but that I had to come right then.

I called school, got a sub for my morning classes, and drove right over.

GB was sitting in the breakfast room. As usual he was beautifully groomed: He smelled delicious when I gave him his smooch and he had on his "hair," the usual beautifully tailored trousers, perky plaid shirt—just everything as I'd always ever known it. And he was *so* happy to unexpectedly see me.

We chatted for a minute, and then, as if nothing had ever changed, he returned to his breakfast while I had a cup of coffee and read different articles to him from the morning paper. Then it was time for him to go. He seemed, in spite of slowing down a bit, as positive and in control as ever, so I left feeling confident that everything was going to be okay.

Daniel called me later to tell me that they had detected fluid on the brain, which was going to have to be drained to relieve the pressure that was causing the problems. Now I was scared again.

Every day passed so slowly. Every time the phone rang my heart stopped. Only his immediate family was allowed to see him, so I wasn't allowed at the hospital.

My life right then was in such turmoil. I was teaching summer school at Immaculate Heart, preparing to move from the very large house my husband, sons, and I had shared to an apartment nearby. This required me to downscale my material possessions and simultaneously work my emotional way through the deterioration of my second marriage.

Eventually, after GB was released from the hospital, I was allowed to come and spend a "little bit of time." As I drove over, wondering what to expect, I realized what "little bit of time" might be remaining. It was this first visit when I was finally allowed to see him that my own life seemed to come back into focus. Seeing him sitting there in his room with his aura of vitality and resiliency restored my own.

■ ■ ■ ■ ■ ■ ■ ■ ■ ■ ■ ■ ■ ■ ■

September 1994

It had been nearly two months since the accident, and although I'd come by, it wasn't until this visit that I would have my first dinner with him during this period. It wasn't that Arlette wouldn't offer me something to eat, but with GB's diet it really meant that she would have had to prepare two dinners. And at this point she and Daniel had more than enough to do. But GB had finally insisted that the next time I came to visit we should eat together.

The first thing I told him when I got there was that school had started for the fall and I was beginning my fifth year of teaching literature. He slowly shook his head as he smiled and said, "You like school, don't you, Kid?"

"Yeah, I really do. I liked going to school and I like teaching school."

"I still don't get it. I always thought, and I still do, that you loved show business."

With that we were right back at each other with the same old shtick. I picked it up with the usual, "I do love show business but I've always loved you more and it was just a way to be with you!"

His surgery had obviously been a success because without missing a beat he hit me with, "Then why did you leave me—twice?"

"Because you're the one who encouraged me to be independent and resilient and know how to take care of myself. And in spite of what you've said, you've never really let me do that!"

"Kid, I don't get you."

"GB, I may have moved out twice and married twice. But have I ever really *left* you?"

"No."

I continued, but a little more gently, "GB, being with you has always been the best. But you love show business the best and I've learned to love other things. Not as much as I love you. But you've pretty much made me what I am. Anyway, there will never be anything as good as being with you."

We just sat there and looked at each other, waiting to see who was going to keep it going.

"Well, Kid, you've defeated me."

"You know, GB, teaching school is really sort of like show business. You get dressed and put on makeup, you've got an audience, you do your performance, while always looking for ways to improve your material for the next time. You hope that somebody got something out of it all, and then you exit but instead of them giving *you* a grade, you give *them* a grade!"

"Kid, maybe you've been in school too long because I have no idea what you're talking about. But if it makes you happy . . ."

"It does."

"Because all I've ever wanted is for you to be happy."

"I know that, GB. You know that I know that. Why else would you have gone to bat for me all those times? Coming to school for me and letting me interview you in front of that awful performance theory class, coming to my piano recitals. All that support has been one of your biggest gifts to me."

"I'll never understand those piano recitals. . . ."

"Hey! After dinner I'll play 'Maple Leaf Rag.'"

"Kid, after dinner I'm going to let you go home and I'm going to bed."

And that was just what we did. In fact, all our dinners to come in all the months that followed involved reliving the past in the best way possible. And after twenty-five years, that was okay. The two of us—me a schoolteacher and him with an old triple-bypass and a lethal knot on his head—sitting in the summer porch having cocktails and the same old arguments. Still loving one another. Could anything have been better?

■ ■ ■ ■ ■ ■ ■ ■ ■ ■ ■ ■ ■ ■

November 1994

During a visit that November I gingerly reminded GB that it was just two decades ago that I'd returned to his house unannounced from Paris after leaving Albin there to continue studying music.

GB shook his head and said, "Kid, you're something else."

"I guess so. I came for a couple of weeks and stayed for two more years!"

"Kinda like, '. . . I'm not saying yes or no—I'm staying five more years!'"

"Oh, nuts, GB! What's that the punchline for? I can't remember the joke!"

"Sure you can, Kid!"

"No, no, no, you tell me one more time and I promise I'll never forget it again."

"You better be sure about that because I may only have one more time to tell it."

"I don't think that's very funny."

"Well, then, let me try the joke. There's this husband and wife and the wife's brother's been living with them for about five years and her husband has had enough. So he says to her, "When 'he' comes down to dinner, you say the soup's too hot and I'll say the soup's too cold. If he agrees with you I'll tell him to get out, and if he agrees with me you tell him to get out. She says fine. The brother comes down for dinner later on, and when the soup's on the table she says, 'This soup's too hot.' And the husband says, 'This soup's too cold.' And the brother says, 'I'm not saying yes or no—I'm staying five more years!'"

"GB, I just love that joke."

I waited a moment and then decided to go ahead and do what I had planned before I came over.

"I brought one of my favorite letters that you wrote to me while I was living in Paris." I asked him if he wanted me to read this twenty-year-old letter, though I knew he'd say yes. And he did say yes—but would I mind reading it to him in English?

"GB, that shouldn't be too hard—you wrote it to me in English."

"Kid, sometimes you really have no sense of humor. Come on, let's hear some of this *facocktah* letter before dinner gets here."

"Okey-doke, but I'm just going to read you the part where you and the guys in the office have come up with a scheme to help me get into show business—again."

"Well, is now too soon because otherwise you're going to kill a season telling me what you're getting ready to do."

I hastily started:

October 21, 1975

This is an idea that might work for you. We'll just give you the outline, and you explain it in your own words when you go on the interview so it will sound natural:

Tell them you were born in Long Beach, the schools you went to, the acting classes, and all your life you wanted to be in show business. Then you worked with the Kids Next Door, you were on the bill with me in Las Vegas, I liked the way you worked, and then you started working with me. Tell him how you appeared in Las Vegas with me, on the Bob Hope TV show, "The Jackie Gleason Show," the talk shows, etc. Then you got married and went to New York to live, but you still took singing, acting, and dancing lessons. Then you did an off-Broadway show--but you still couldn't get that big break, the right door just

wouldn't open for you. Then when your husband
went to Paris you got an idea; you'd go to Paris,
learn to speak French fluently, then come back to
America, speak English with a French accent, and be
discovered as another Fifi D'Orsay, who became a
star just that way. In the meantime while you're in
Paris if they need an American actress you could
always speak French with an American accent.
However, when you go back to America, if the door
still doesn't open, then you might go to Spain, and
try the same thing. And if that doesn't work, you'll
try Italy, Germany, even Russia. But you're positive
that sooner or later you're going to return to
America as a foreign star.

Well, that's my brainstorm, and I think it's a good one.
Maybe you can develop it further. . . .

"Well, did it work?"

"I never tried it out. I came back here right after that letter and went back to
school."

"Maybe we'd better eat our dinner so . . . you can get back to school."

■ ■ ■ ■ ■ ■ ■ ■ ■ ■ ■ ■ ■ ■ ■

December 1994

Because the letter had been such a success and we'd had such a good time, I decided that—since we were in the middle of the Christmas season—I would bring a selection of Christmas pictures from over the years that I'd saved. I thought I'd see what kind of a mood he was in before I did anything. If he seemed up, I'd bring them out. If he seemed low, we could certainly talk about other things.

When I got there everything was just as it had been for years, even though we had always been and still were "The Christmas Curmudgeon Couple." The summer porch was all Christmasy. GB looked terrific in a tartan plaid flannel shirt and big smile.

He waited for me to give him a smooch.

"Hey, Kid, whatcha got there?"

He pointed to my knitting bag with the envelope of pictures sticking out of it.

"I brought you some old Christmas pictures."

As I leaned over him, he stopped and looked at me. We were nose to nose.

"What, no case of ketchup this year?"

"What, no diamond ring this year?"

"Are you going to knit or are we going to look at those pictures?" This didn't require an answer. "Fix yourself a drink and freshen mine up, and get my reading glasses for me."

As I did as I was told, I quietly said to him, "*Please* would be nice."

"Lots of ice and not too much Vermouth . . . *please.*"

I sat on the floor at his feet and we looked at the pictures together. It was amazing that he looked pretty much the same. What a guy!

The last set of pictures we looked at that night were from a Christmas party just a few years earlier that Paul and I had given for over a hundred people! GB had come with Barry Mirkin and held court in our library in front of the fireplace. At one point during the party someone hit the alarm system emergency button and an ambulance came screaming up as we sat there. GB looked out the huge window in the library at the flashing lights outside and said, "That must be for me! I guess it's time to exit!"

There was also a great picture of him sitting and eating a huge plate of food.

"For someone who doesn't care much about food, you really ate up a storm!"

"Kid, I got a TL for you. (TL is an old show biz expression for trade-last: I'll pay you a compliment and then you pay me one—sort of a "gotcha last.") You turned out to be a great cook!"

"Well, then, I got a TL for you! You're still the nicest man I'll ever know!"

With perfect timing, Daniel came in to tell us dinner was ready.

"Come on, Kid, we don't want the soup to get cold!"

It was time to go eat some more.

■ ■ ■ ■ ■ ■ ■ ■ ■ ■ ■ ■ ■ ■

January 1995

We were into the new year and approaching GB's birthday. Ninety-nine! He was so amazing—and if what I'd been taught in college about survival instincts and man's basic drives panned out, I knew he was going to make it to 100 for sure!

But at that particular time I wasn't so sure about my own longevity.

That New Year's had been particularly depressing. I'd spent it alone, and here I was—dining with GB with not a positive thought or story to tell. It used to be that when I felt blue and joined him for dinner, I could tell GB everything that was bothering me, and even though he'd be sympathetic and supportive as always, he'd sort of "jerked a knot in my psychic tail," gave me a reality check, and set me back on course. But now he had enough on his plate, and I knew he was probably preoccupied with his upcoming birthday plans.

New Year's 1976 at the Backuses.

I plodded in, dragging my own self-pity. I gave poor ol' GB a thoughtless kiss and plopped myself down opposite him.

"What's up Kid?"

"Nuthin'."

"What'd you do for New Year's?"

"Nuthin'. I was alone." (Oh poor me, poor miserable me!)

"That was your choice. I asked you to go with me to Henny Backus's. We've only gone there for years!"

"Yeah, I know. I just didn't feel like going out."

"Well, you could have gotten over yourself and gone out with me since we've always gone out for New Year's whenever we've been alone at the same time."

"GB, I'm sorry and you're right. I've made my own misery."

He just sat and gave me "the glint" and waited for me to say something else.

"GB, you're right, we've always had a great time at New Year's. In fact, I still have that fabulous gypsy dress you bought me that I wore to the Harold Robbins party at Gatsby's restaurant. I suppose I could have put that dress on and had a glass of champagne by myself, but I didn't."

"First of all, Kid, you'll have to take off a few pounds if you're ever going to put that dress on again, so forget the champagne."

I wasn't up for that conversation.

"GB, I'll take this weight off pretty soon. I just don't want to think about it now."

"Why? Is now too soon? You don't take off a few pounds, you'll spend next New Year's alone, too."

With that last comment the tears just started rolling down my face. There was only one Achilles' heel GB ever had—tears. The last thing I wanted to do was upset him.

He gently reached across the table and took my hands in his still smooth, tan, and beautiful hands and gave them a squeeze.

"Kid, what are you trying to do? Teach yourself a lesson?"

With that old line I finally started to laugh and we were back on an even keel for the rest of the visit.

■ ■ ■ ■ ■ ■ ■ ■ ■ ■ ■ ■ ■ ■ ■

February 1995

I was warned as soon as I came in the kitchen that GB was not in a good mood. Uh-oh. He had said he didn't want any dinner and I should come right upstairs when I got there. GB on the warpath—*not* fun. He was probably just really tired.

Ever since he'd started feeling better he'd really been on the go. In and out of the office, going to Hillcrest, rehearsing at the house, going out for Thursday night dinners when Daniel and Arlette were off. Except, of course, by now Daniel and Arlette never took the same days off because one of them would always need to be with him. Daniel almost always accompanied him wherever he went.

I took a deep breath and started upstairs. Show time!

"Hey, GB."

"Hiya, Kid."

"Wanna watch some football?"

"Nope, I wanna go back to bed."

"Well, you can't. You have to eat your dinner first."

"I'm not hungry."

"Doesn't make any difference. Ya gotta eat something."

He gave me an almost dirty look and I nonchalantly took out my knitting.

"Well, if I'm going to eat, then where is it?"

"Daniel's on his way up with dinner."

He sat and silently watched me knitting while I scoured my brain for a positive topic of conversation.

I stopped and looked right at him. "Well, GB, if you could have anything you wanted to eat, what would it be?"

"It doesn't make any difference because it all tastes the same and I don't care about food anyway."

It was the same old thing about how food was never too important to him. For someone to whom food was never important, he sure had always been fussy about what he ate: "If you can carry the soup to the table, it's not hot enough."

For years he'd always "suggested" what I should order when we were out. For years he had my birthday parties in one of the rooms at Chasen's if not in the front room and he always ordered the same menu: cracked crab to start, Hobo steak with puffed potatoes, spinach salad, and flaming orange-flavored vodka martinis. At the 21 in New York it was always the turkey burgers. At the old Brown Derby was the Cobb salad.

By now his dinner had arrived and he was putting ketchup and even salt (!) on everything! Then he started to pick at his food and move it around on his plate. Finally, I told him he'd never guess what I'd been thinking about and I went back to my knitting. He sat waiting for me to continue and I knew I had him with a really obscure piece of information.

"I bet you're glad you're not eating that recipe that you submitted to that cookbook from the '30s."

"Kid, what the hell are you talking about?"

"I'm talking about that cookbook you gave me years ago from your library called *What Actors Eat, When They Eat!* It has all sorts of recipes from the stars during the '30s that they all claim to be their favorite thing to eat."

"Mine must have been ketchup soup."

"Nope."

"Okay, I know you're dying to tell me. What was it?"

"It's a recipe for creamed chicken and peas in patty shells."

"I would never eat that kind of *drek*!"

"No, but you said you did and I still remember the recipe because I believed it and one time I tried to make it."

"Then how does it go?"

"Not so good!"

"What's it got in it? I must have gotten it from one of our cooks."

Here's the recipe exactly as it appears in the book:

Creamed Chicken and Peas in Patty Shells

2 tbsp. butter
2 tbsp. flour
1 cup milk
¼ tsp. salt

1 cup diced chicken
(1 small can)
1 cup fresh cooked peas
1 egg yolk beaten

Melt butter, blend with flour, add milk and salt. Cook about fifteen minutes. Then add chicken and peas, cooking until they are hot--add two tablespoons of milk to the beaten egg yolk and stir into the mixture. Cook two minutes, fill patty shells--to serve four. (CONTINUED NEXT PAGE)

Patty Shells

1½ cup pastry flour   4½ tbsp. ice water
½ tsp. salt
½ cup shortening

Chill flour and shortening in refrigerator. Sift flour and salt together into bowl. Cut in shortening with two knives until mixture resembles coarse meal. Add ice water gradually--just enough to make stiff dough. Cover bowl and chill in refrigerator overnight, or at least one hour.

Place pastry on floured board and roll lightly from center a little less than one-eighth inch thick. Cut in circles to cover inverted three-inch muffin tins, flute edges, and prick--or line three-inch fluted patty and press in another patty shell, letting it remain for half of baking period. Bake either kind of patty shell for twelve minutes in hot (450 degrees) oven until light brown. Makes twelve patty shells.

"Kid, I don't believe I ever ate anything like that, let alone knew how to make it. Cream sauce? Pastry shells? Peas? I wouldn't use peas to put my cigar out in!"

"I don't believe you ever made it either, but I know you used to eat stuff like that because I have the picture from Hawaii of you in your bathing suit right around this time and you were packing a few pounds."

"Kid, I went on a diet then, lost the weight, and have kept it off ever since! Should I keep going?"

I knew where he was going so I changed the subject—fast.

I went back to my knitting and slowly recounted all the good restaurants we'd eaten in over the years while he slowly started eating his dinner. By the time I'd finished my litany of dining experiences, he'd finished his dinner and was waiting for his cookies, ice cream, and tea.

"Well, Kid, we did it!"

"Yeah, GB, and it wasn't easy!"

"And neither are you!"

▪ ▪ ▪ ▪ ▪ ▪ ▪ ▪ ▪ ▪ ▪ ▪ ▪ ▪

April 1995

It was the first Monday in April. The annual Academy Awards ceremony was being held. I can't remember an occasion when we didn't watch the Oscars together and I'll never forget when we actually attended them together.

This night, I got to the house a bit early so I could watch the pre-Oscar interviews. I figured I'd just watch it alone on the summer porch until GB awoke and then I'd go on upstairs. When I got there, Arlette told me GB was already up and waiting for me! With pictures in hand, I hustled up the back stairs.

GB was sitting at his desk with the TV going full blast.

"Hey, GB! It was just nineteen years ago today!"

"And isn't it nice that we can sit here and have hot soup and enjoy ourselves?"

"Aw, come on, you know it was fun. I brought the pictures to prove it!"

I pulled out the pictures of the movie premiere of *The Sunshine Boys* and the pictures of us leaving the house to go to the awards ceremony.

"Y'know, GB, you still look pretty much the same except, of course, now you have your pajamas on."

He gave me the "glint" and informed me I was still a "fresh kid" and that I should be quiet because the show was back on.

When dinner came up, he told me he'd had enough and to turn the volume down. I didn't question it because I had the feeling that he found it slightly depressing.

As we ate our dinner, he asked me what was going on. The only thing I could think of to report was the forthcoming Easter vacation ski trip on which Paul was taking Nathaniel, Ben, and me.

"Kid, I don't get it. You're still married and still vacation together but you don't live together."

"I've told you that I have no impulse control, and that if I divorced Paul, I'd probably get married yet again."

"Well, this time I probably won't be available!"

Every now and then, GB would make these pointed references to his health, and it gave me great waves of *Weltschmerz,* German for melancholy or great feelings of "world-pain," which would fill my chest to bursting for a moment.

As GB got back to his dinner, he told me to go over to the table and get the copy of a new *Life* magazine that was there. The issue featured celebrities and their cats. It ran a really terrific picture of Willie the cat on the breakfast table with CB; they both looked perfect. It was a scene I'd seen so many times over the years with GB and his different kitties: this meticulous man allowing these felines right up there in his food!

"GB, you sure have always spoiled your kitties!"

He gave me a slow smile and answered, "You never complained before."

"And I'm not complaining now."

GB looked up at me as I was leaning over him looking at the magazine and continued, "Kid, what are we doing looking at pictures of cats and talking about . . ."

"GB, don't even say it!"

"Since you already know all my jokes, let's go back to the Oscars and have some cookies and ice cream."

And so we did.

But I must admit that, later on, as I was leaving, I stopped for a minute in the library and looked at his Oscar. I went over and touched it and thought to myself that once again on Academy Awards night I was getting to touch a real live Oscar. Twice in one life . . . am I lucky or what?

■ ■ ■ ■ ■ ■ ■ ■ ■ ■ ■ ■ ■ ■ ■

July 1995

Another Fourth of July. I wondered if GB was going to make George Washington jokes.

When I got up to GB's room I had a sudden rush of déjà vu. The room was familiarly calm and comforting and still looked as it had since I'd had it redone all those years ago in the summer of '73. GB looked reassuringly stable and happy to see me. The windows were open and there was an imperceptible breeze blowing through the room and wafting on the breeze was the faint scent of cordite—in other words, gunpowder.

"Hate to disappoint you, GB, but I didn't bring any fireworks."

"I thought about you and your fireworks when I smelled that smell outside."

"GB, it was more like US and the fireworks!"

"It was more like your brother Graham, your girlfriend Susan, and *you* and the fireworks. I just watched."

"But *you* bought them."

"You're still the one who set the pool and the orange trees on fire!"

"It's not too late. You could put on your hair and we could go buy some right now."

"That's one trip I don't think I'll be making again."

Oh, *Weltschmerz* time again.

"GB, it's still not too late for a little Fourth of July action."

"Kid, you make a mistake once, it's a learning thing. You make the same mistake twice, you're stupid!" He paused and then continued, "And I'm not just talking about the fireworks."

"You win. Let's eat our dinner. It may not be as hot as that Fourth of July."

". . . and neither am I," he says.

■ ■ ■ ■ ■ ■ ■ ■ ■ ■ ■ ■ ■ ■ ■

September 1995

I got there to find trouble. GB was up in his room and very unhappy. He was sitting at his desk for drinks and dinner but he was being uncharacteristically crabby. Nothing was right. He complained he wasn't straight in his chair and he couldn't seem to get straightened out. His wonderful nurse, Velma, was unsuccessfully trying to straighten him up in the chair.

"I'm not in the MIDDLE!"

She gently adjusted him so he was sitting perfectly.

I reassured him, "Poppa, now you're straight in the middle."

"No, I'm not straight in the middle."

We looked at each other. He seemed embarrassed to be pitching a fit in front of me, but he obviously didn't feel well. I wasn't quite sure how tough to be, so I waited to get a reading from him on how he really was. He looked at me to see my reaction.

He continued, "I'll never be straight in the middle again. I'm just in the middle, and in the middle of nowhere now that I think about it!"

"Well, if you're in the middle of nowhere, then you're somewhere."

Our eyes locked. I didn't know what that was supposed to mean but it was what I thought.

GB had recently had a relapse and it really hit him hard. It hit all of us hard. From what I could gather, he'd been back to rehabilitation and was starting to go back into the office and the club for lunch and cards, and to enjoy his Thursday night dinners out. But he seemed to be getting tinier and tinier, and now sometimes he didn't want to get out of bed and it was all I could do to keep him amused when I came to visit.

I still brought pictures and thought up some of the old stories, maybe coerced him into singing some of his really obscure songs that always made me laugh and made him concentrate. Sometimes it seemed that he would rather just sit and listen to me babble on about some inanity or mundane event in my life. He enjoyed the companionship.

I finally realized that he was waiting for me to say something. Oh yeah! I got it! Rosh Hashanah and Yom Kippur were coming soon, so I asked him to sing "When It's Rosh Hashanah Time in Dixieland."

The first time I had ever heard GB sing this, Jack Benny had asked him to sing it. I've never seen anyone get so tickled. He started to laugh as soon as GB opened his mouth.

"Kid, I don't think I can remember it."

"Sure you can. If you sing that I'll sing 'Aunt Jemima' to you."

"You don't know all the words to 'Aunt Jemima.'"

"Sure I do, and I'll even get up at the chorus and do the cakewalk."

I could tell he wasn't quite sure if I was serious or not.

". . . and when I'm all through I'll do the splits and kick the back of my head."

With my last comment he started to sing. Velma stopped what she was doing to listen and pretty soon we were laughing our heads off. He did the whole complicated song and then waited for me.

"Okay, now let's see you top Tess Gardell."

"I didn't say I could top Tess Gardell. I only said I could sing her song!"
And I started:

> *Hello everybody don't you know my name,*
> *I'm Aunt Jemima of the pancake fame.*
> *See me on the billboards everywhere.*
> *See me in the subways here and there.*

With this the tempo of the song changes and slowly, in time with the music, I started to get out of my chair, and GB smiled at me warily.

> *The pancake business—*
> *It was getting slow,*
> *So I took my pancake bakers*
> *And went to make some dough.*

Cakewalk time!

> *Because I'm Aunt (step/kick) Jemima (step/kick)*

I finished the song as I "step/kicked" around him.

> *And my five bakers,*
> *We're all ragtime shimmy shakers.*
> *We got kind of tired of the place*
> *Where we was at,*

So we all walked out
And left the pancakes flat!
The boys were good at baking
But also shimmy shaking.
That you know you can't deny
You can't deny!
So the boys all got up when the
Band began to play,
And everybody there they started
Swingin' and to sway!
Because I'm Aunt Jemima
And my five bakers,
We're ragtime shimmy shakers now!

"Kid, sit down before you hurt yourself!"

"So?"

"So you only loused up a few of the lyrics. I'd stick to teaching if I was you!"

With this last comment, he started on his dinner.

He seemed a little bit better and ate his whole dinner, which was encouraging. But as soon as he finished, he demanded to go to bed. I knew I should try to keep him up for at least another half hour. The bed! I remembered a story about the bed that I was sure he'd forgotten.

"GB, remember when you had twin beds in here when I first met you?"

He waited to see what sort of obscure foolishness I was going to bring up now.

"Do you remember that time Bobby Darin came to stay for a couple of weeks while there was some work being done on his house?"

"Kid, I'm getting tired. This better have a funny finish."

"Don't you remember what I did to him?"

"Kid, I have trouble remembering what I did to *you*!"

"You guys slept in here and I slept in my room but we'd all watch TV in here at night and you two would get in the beds and I'd sit on the floor at the foot of your bed and the two of you would tease me the whole time we were watching TV."

"I remember now, Kid. After about a week, one night you short-sheeted the beds."

"Pretty funny, huh?"

"Oh yeah, a laugh riot."

"There you two were, trying to get your legs in your beds, and neither of you would admit that anything was wrong until in the middle of your struggling I started laughing. That sure put an end to your teasing!"

"That it did. And now I'm gonna put an end to you! I want to go to bed. So I'm gonna let you go home."

He looked at me for a minute and said with a deadpan expression, "I certainly hope that's not the kind of stuff you did in bed with either of your husbands!"

With that I gave him his smooch and started to leave.

"Kid, next week when you come, why don't you bring some more pictures? That way you won't have to sing—and neither will I!"

I just knew he was going to make it to 100!

· SIXTEEN ·

When I saw GB next, I thought I would probably never see him again. Or at least never again in as good a condition as I had for the previous year and a half of his illness. The thought of this was more than I could bear for a number of reasons.

First of all, this took place at Hillcrest Country Club. For nearly a year, I'd only visited with him at the house while he was upstairs wearing his pajamas and having his dinner. But on this day, I'd asked the privilege of using the Hillcrest for lunch because GB's current biographer, Martin Gottfried, whom I'd met the previous May, was in town and had expressed an interest in sampling the famous brunch that Hillcrest offers every Sunday.

This request had been difficult in itself. Normally I would not have included Mr. Gottfried since he was not a close mutual friend of ours and therefore not welcome in what I considered to be one of our inner sanctums. But I concluded, in spite of everything, that Mr. Gottfried was "okay" because he seemed to be so very fond and admiring of his subject during the five months when we first spoke.

Initially when Mr. Gottfried had called me I refused to divulge anything about GB, telling him that anything GB wanted the public to know he would have written himself years ago. I also had been advised by those around GB that I should speak to no one—with the silent subtext being "if you know what's good for you." But, because of Mr. Gottfried's professional credentials and seeming lack of guile, I eventually had acquiesced and in these past five months had imparted bits of information that I thought would be essential for what I was convinced would be the definitive and psychologically insightful biography of someone I loved so much—although I must admit that at times I'd had very mixed feelings about disclosing things that I knew GB had only shared or discussed with me, or when giving updates on the current status of GB's physical and mental condition.

When Mr. Gottfried and I arrived at the club, GB's longtime friend and companion, Barry Mirkin, greeted us. He said that GB was in the card room and that when Daniel wheeled him out to go home, he'd bring him over to say hello.

As we sat having lunch I saw, over Mr. Gottfried's shoulder, Daniel and Barry coming out of the card room. The reality of the situation was like a sharp kick in my stomach and literally left me breathless and faint. GB was in a wheelchair and looked no bigger than Ben, my seven-year-old son. He was, as always, beautifully groomed but his clothes literally hung on him and then draped over the sides of the wheelchair. His face was waxen and his eyes were confusedly rolling in his head as he tried to figure out who he was supposed to be looking for, or maybe even where he was.

I hurried over to him, calling, "Poppa, it's Lisa, I'm here." I knelt and took his hands in mine, stared into his eyes, and for a brief moment the thin swirling blue film over them seemed to solidify and we made eye contact. He looked at me with a sweet expectancy and I thanked him for allowing me to come to the club. Mr. Gottfried had now joined me, so I introduced them even though they had met several years earlier for an interview. GB shakily extended his tiny hand and said, "Nice to see you."

I told him I'd see him soon at the house and Daniel gently wheeled him out toward the car.

My eyes had filled with tears before I'd even returned to the table. I realized that everyone in the dining room was looking at us and that I was not going to be able to continue, so I excused myself.

I went into the ladies' room and wept. I wept for myself and the loss that seemed to be rapidly approaching. I wept for Poppa because when I'd looked into his eyes I realized that he and I both knew, and there was nothing we could do. I wept because I felt like I had really overstepped my bounds and certainly made a bad judgment call by including an outsider in our private life, especially at this point in time.

■ ■ ■ ■ ■ ■ ■ ■ ■ ■ ■ ■ ■ ■ ■

The week after this encounter, Arlette kept me posted on how GB was, and it wasn't good. He wouldn't even get out of bed, let alone go to the office or Hillcrest.

I was so scared. I was as scared as I'd been the first time I went to see him after the accident. But I knew that I must go visit him. And I went.

And it was terrific!

It was so absolutely mind-bogglingly miraculous and wonderful that I was giddy for the next twenty-four hours.

At first he didn't want to get up for the nurse, so Arlette came downstairs and got me. His tiny body was curled up in his bed in a fetal position. I leaned over the bed and gave him a big kiss on the cheek, explaining who I was.

He recognized me. That was good.

He told me he was going to stay in bed while I dined. I explained to him that *he* was the one who was going to have dinner, so he needed to get up and get ready. The glint. The familiar glint in his eyes—which he saved for me—appeared. The watery blue eyes became sharp and he told me I was going to have to move if he was going to get out of bed. Yes! We're on our way!

As I sat across from him at the desk, I couldn't believe what I saw. He had color in his face. He was alert as Arlette cut up his food. His hands were steady. He looked over at me and our eyes met and we gave each other enormous grins. He smiled and said, "Kid, we're still booked."

The rest of the evening only got better. As he ate, I started chatting. The cookies came and our old joke.

"GB, can you eat that whole plate of cookies all alone?"

"No, but with you I could!"

What a sweet new punchline to our favorite joke. I told him about rereading all the letters he had written to me for those three years when I didn't live in Los Angeles and how funny and warm and loving they were and how I cherished them.

Then I took a chance. I told him the letters reminded me of some of the vaudeville stories he'd told me that he'd never told in public. The "glint" reappeared.

"Like what?"

"Like the gingersnap story." I could tell that he didn't really remember.

"You know, Poppa, the one where you weren't an opening act but you were still playing small-time theaters so you had to share a dressing room with another single act."

"Remind me of it again, Kid."

So I did.

It seems that the fella GB shared the dressing room with was a slob. And not just a slob but a dirty slob. Since the dressing room was very small—with just a sink, a rod on which to hang the wardrobe, and a communal dressing table—there was no escaping this guy and his filthy habits. Some of these habits included spitting and "wee-weeing" (as GB always put it) in the sink! This was where they had to brush their teeth and wash their faces after taking off their makeup! This guy was driving GB nuts and he finally decided he had to do something about it.

GB went out and bought a bag of gingersnap cookies, waited until this guy was out of the dressing room, went in the dressing room, took a gingersnap cookie, moistened it sufficiently, and gently mashed it into the tail of one of the shirts that was hanging on the wardrobe rack.

By the time the fella returned, the cookies had dried and taken on an appearance of something other than a cookie. As he came in the dressing room, he stopped dead cold and stared at the tail of the shirt as GB sat quietly, putting on his makeup for the next performance. "Whose is this?" the actor demanded. GB casually got up, went over to the shirt, snapped off a piece of gingersnap, popped it in his mouth, savored it for a moment, and responded while smacking his lips, "It's mine." With this, the actor scooped up his makeup, yanked "his" shirt from the rack, and ran like a thief! GB had the dressing room to himself after that.

As I finished the story, GB's face lit up with recognition. "Yeah, that fella really was a dirty son-of-a-bitch!" No, this was not the man I'd seen at Hillcrest the week before! At this point he looked at me expectantly. He wanted more. There were plenty of stories for me to choose from.

"GB, remember the wee-wee stories?"

"Kid, I can't even pee on my shoes."

"You know what I mean."

He expectantly looked at me again.

"Well, there are the two stories I remember when you were a skating act and the stage was raked." (A raked stage is one that is built with a slant down toward the audience.)

GB kept looking at me for more.

"The first raked stage story I remember was when you were hired as a skating act. They forget to tell you that the stage was raked." He's waiting.

"So you skated out to do your act, unaware that it was raked, and you hadn't locked the front wheels on your skates. You could barely keep yourself from rolling into the footlights as you tried to dance."

"That's right! I couldn't stop myself and had to keep skating on the bias!" (This means across the stage rather than up and downstage.) "But what about the time me and that jerky fella were doing the skating act on a raked stage?"

That was the other story.

"We were going to do our act. And at the last minute my partner had to wee-wee. But we were supposed to go on stage so I told him to go pee in the cuspidor in the corner. Unfortunately, we both forgot it was a raked stage, so when he went and peed in the corner offstage and he missed the cuspidor, it hit the floor and rolled down toward the audience!"

GB always remembered this story. I let him continue because I'd always loved to hear it.

"He wee-weed and it rolled right down and under the curtain and down the raked stage and into the footlights, which proceeded to explode when the water hit them. They burst and the smoke was awful and they had to air out the theater before we could go on. What a putz! I don't think me and that guy worked together after that!"

"GB, don't forget the 'biting bear' story!"

"The 'biting bear'?"

"Yeah. Remember? You were working with trained bears and you were sort of nervous. So you asked the trainer about the bears."

"Oh, yeah! He told me not to worry. He pointed to the bears and told me how well-behaved they were. The trainer said to me as he pointed to a particular bear,

'This bear here is the most tame of all.' And as he pointed at the bear, it leaned over and bit off the end of his index finger."

"But, GB, don't forget my favorite story about Dainty Marie."

"Oh, Kid, not the Dainty Marie story."

"Yeah, Dainty Marie. Just one more story, Poppa, and then I'll go home."

"And where's home?"

We stopped for a moment and looked at each other.

"It's always with you. But give me Dainty Marie."

"For you, Kid! So Dainty Marie did a 'quiet rope' act. And this night she had one of her new boyfriends holding her rope for her." The act was a straight rope act in which the performer worked a rope that had to be held taut at the bottom so that she could do her routine on a single rope. It included a series of very graceful contortions and an aerial display.

"Well, at this performance, Dainty Marie gracefully climbed to the top of the rope as her latest flame held the rope taut. Unfortunately, they'd had a very large Italian dinner earlier, so when Dainty Marie went to do the splits as he was down below, she let go of some of her dinner, and with that a 'blue flame shot out of her heinie' and her new boyfriend ran like a thief. There she was, whirling and twirling around on this loose rope. That was the end of her act for the night!"

After GB had finished this last story, he reached his hands across the table and took my hands in his. "I love you, Kid," he said. "And now I gotta scrub my teeth and go to bed so I can get up again. I'm gonna let you go."

"Oh, please, just one more."

There was a pause as we looked at each other. I could tell he was tired but I was going to be really selfish.

"GB—the 'wow-wow mouth' story."

"Kid, why do you remember all this *drek*?"

"Because it's not *drek* to me! Come on."

"Okay, okay."

The "wow-wow mouth" story is about GB and Jack Benny and a minstrel show in which they performed. For the finale, all the vaudeville acts came out and participated in a minstrel show. Now that I think about it, it was probably the last of the great minstrel shows. Too bad! Anyway, all the headliners put on blackface makeup and minstrel costumes for the end of the show. The makeup was inspired by the cartoon character Bosco, with that big white area left around the mouth so that it looked really big.

Because GB was always out to make Mr. Benny laugh, he decided that for every show, when he put on his makeup, he would leave more and more white area around his mouth. And every show, when Mr. Benny looked at him and saw the makeup, he would start laughing on stage, which was just what GB wanted. Eventually, the white area left for the mouth extended completely around GB's *ears*! And on that night when GB's "wow-wow mouth" extended completely around his ears, he looked at Mr. Benny, who was already a laughing wreck, and slowly peeled off his gloves—which was what the minstrel performers did at the end of the show to show that they were really white!

"Kid, I gotta let you go!"

And I gave him a smooch and I went.

As I walked down the back stairs to the kitchen, my whole being filled with a profound sense of faith and hope. His birthday was only two months away. I thought there was a possibility I still might be able to give him this birthday book in person.

"But, just in case I can't, GB," I thought to myself as I got in the car to go home, "let me say now, an early Happy Birthday!" I finished my little birthday prayer to him with, "GB, you're still right. You're the nicest man I'll ever know. And thank you for making every day of my life seem like my birthday!"

■ ■ ■ ■ ■ ■ ■ ■ ■ ■ ■ ■ ■ ■

December 1995

The last time I visited GB was December 23, 1995. He was completely preoccupied with the fact that he was going to Frank Sinatra's house for Christmas Eve dinner and he would be asked to perform. What was he to sing?

"Poppa, what about 'The Doggies in the Street'?"

"How's it go, Kid? And don't tell me 'good.'"

"Okay, okay."

Nathaniel doing his imitation of Poppa in GB's star chair.

The doggies in the street
Get together and play
Talk things over . . .
Get married right away.
The chicken laid the egg
The egg can't be found!
And Mr. Rooster
Doesn't come around.

The ants get married
Every time they get a chance.
So do their brothers and their
Sisters and their aunts.
And the bull couldn't live
Without the female cow—
The cat couldn't live
Without the cat's MEOW!

"Kid, I don't think that's what I want to sing. Maybe you can sing it to Ben and Nathaniel on Christmas Eve!"

"Thanks a lot, GB. I just figured it was short and sweet."

"Kid, I wouldn't touch that line."

Well, at least he was starting to feel a little perkier than when I arrived.

"I know. How about 'I Forgot the Number of My House'?"

"Sing it with me."

> *Oh, I forgot the number of my house*
> *The last time I went out.*
> *Oh, I forgot the number of my house*
> *And for hours I roamed about*
> *ALL ALONE!*
> *But I've unscrewed the number*
> *From the door!*
> *And I've got it here tonight!*
> *So all I need to find is the door that*
> *It belongs on . . .*
> *And I'm all right!*

"Yeah, that's it, GB. Do it!"

"Well, that's over so I'm going to eat my dinner and let you go home to your children! Give the Berry Boys and Paul my love and have a Merry Christmas! I'll talk to you in a couple of days."

"You got it, GB, and I love you."

"I love you, too. You're a nice girl."

That was the last time I ever saw him.

■ ■ ■ ■ ■ ■ ■ ■ ■ ■ ■ ■ ■ ■

GB came down with the flu right after that party, and I developed bronchial pneumonia. I called every day to check on him, knowing that to see him was too risky for us. Finally, I was granted visiting rights, even though he was only allowed visitors for five minutes at a time. The next time he awoke I would be called, and only then should I dash over to the house to spend the allotted five minutes.

I was never given that time. It was revoked in a most abrupt, vindictive, brutal, and terse manner. When I sensed what was going on, I asked over the phone if this meant I wasn't ever going to be allowed to visit again. The response was a smug, "That's right." Then I was given the sage advice, "You'll just have to remember him as he was."

I realized I was being punished not for talking to Martin Gottfried, his biographer, but for being quoted extensively in his book. All my contact with GB was prohibited. I'd become the pariah of the inner circle. All those who ran GB's life had united in one common goal now that GB was unable to be aware of it: to make me as miserable as possible. I was not going to be allowed contact with the person who for the last thirty years was the most important in my life.

■ ■ ■ ■ ■ ■ ■ ■ ■ ■ ■ ■ ■ ■

February 29, 1996

How sad it is when people who love one another, are devoted to each other in a way that need never be explained or defended to others, are suddenly kept apart by outside forces. To have this sort of intimacy invaded and controlled by outsiders who make choices rightfully left to Fate—that's cruel. And to have one's options revoked with no recourse is unbearably painful.

Unfortunately, this was what my thirty years with GB ended with—my exile and a forced physical separation. But our spirits were irrevocably united years ago, and no one could change that.

■ ■ ■ ■ ■ ■ ■ ■ ■ ■ ■ ■ ■ ■ ■

March 9, 1996

GB died this morning. Of course, of course, we all knew he was going to die. But that didn't make it any easier.

It seemed such a very long day. When I'd gone out that morning I never dreamed of the messages I would pick up when I came home.

The first one was from Paul, and when he called me "dear" I knew something was wrong. I assumed Nathaniel, from the tone of Paul's voice, had finally used a dull razor on his younger brother's throat. The next message was from Tonda in New York telling me how sorry she was. I stopped the tape. I knew what had happened. There was only one thing that could make people call me with such somber tones of voice. GB.

I called Paul, and, before he could say anything, I told him GB was gone. He slowly responded, "Yes."

I'd never felt such physical shock in my life. Not after childbirth, not after the realization that a divorce was pending. Nothing will ever compare. A fierce cold swept through my body and stayed in me. Nothing could stop me from shaking and being cold. I couldn't put two thoughts together. The phone started ringing, but holding the receiver was more than I could physically accomplish. I was chilled to my very marrow.

Just the Monday before that I'd given Jack Langdon—who'd become my "Switzerland" since he had remained neutral during the whole recent ruckus—a letter and a lovely silver-framed photo of GB and myself that was one of my favorites, to be given to GB the next time he came into the office.

MARCH 3, 1996

DEAREST GB,

I WAS SO HAPPY TO HEAR ON TV THAT YOU'RE UP AND OUT OF THE HOUSE! ! ! ! !

BUT I'M VERY UNHAPPY THAT I'M NOT BEING ALLOWED TO SEE YOU SO I'VE SENT YOU ONE OF MY FAVORITE PICTURES OF US AND AT LEAST YOU CAN SEE ME EVERY DAY AND KNOW THAT I THINK ABOUT YOU ALL THE TIME AND WILL ALWAYS LOVE YOU.

LIKE YOU'VE ALWAYS TOLD ME, YOU'RE THE NICEST MAN I'LL EVER KNOW! ! ! !

But there was never to be a next time. He would get neither the photograph of us nor the love letter.

As I sat writing this, I choked on tears. I couldn't believe that I really didn't get to see him one last time. And then on TV, there were people in "the business" who never really knew him intimately, giving heartfelt and intimate interviews. It was so distasteful to witness. Show biz.

■ ■ ■ ■ ■ ■ ■ ■ ■ ■ ■ ■ ■ ■ ■

GB spoiled me to death and now he was gone. I would never again have the self-confidence that he gave me. I would never be the brightest or the smartest or the prettiest again, but at least he gave me the illusion that I was for those years we were together. He always made me feel I was so special that I don't think I'll ever know that feeling again. Who knows, maybe being "ordinary" will be easy after thirty years. I've realized that he will always be with me in any logical goodness or straight thinking that guides my life.

I know that no one will ever love me as much as he loved me, but no one will ever love him as much as I've loved him.

Like he always told me: "Kid, I'm the nicest man you'll ever know."

GB, you were right.

I love you and remain,

Always yours